true
purity*

true purity*

*more than just saying "no"
to you-know-what

HAYLEY &
MICHAEL **DiMARCO**

Revell
a division of Baker Publishing Group
Grand Rapids, Michigan

Hungry
Planet

© 2013 by Hungry Planet

Published by Revell
a division of Baker Publishing Group
P.O. Box 6287, Grand Rapids, MI 49516-6287
www.revellbooks.com

Printed in the United States of America

Library of Congress Cataloging-in-Publication Data
DiMarco, Hayley.
    True purity : more than just saying "no" to you-know-what / Hayley DiMarco and Michael DiMarco.
    p. cm.
    Includes bibliographical references.
    ISBN 978-0-8007-2068-1 (pbk.)
    1. Christian teenagers—Religious life. 2. Christian teenagers—Sexual behavior. 3. Sex—Religious aspects—Christianity. 4. Christian teenagers—Conduct of life. I. DiMarco, Michael. II. Title.
    BV4531.3.D5622 2013
    241'.6640835—dc23   2012038207

Published in association with Christopher Ferebee, Literary Agent, Corona, California.

13 14 15 16 17 18 19   7 6 5 4 3 2 1

But
under-
stand
this, that
in the last
days there will
come times of
difficulty. For people
will be lovers of self,
lovers of money, proud,
arrogant, abusive, disobedient
to their parents, ungrateful,
unholy, heartless, unappeasable,
slanderous, without self-control,
brutal, not loving good, treacherous,
reckless, swollen with conceit, lovers
of pleasure rather than lovers of God,
having the appearance of godliness,
but denying its power. Avoid
such people.

2 Timothy 3:1–5 ESV

Contents

Introduction

May the Lord direct your hearts to the love of God and to the steadfastness of Christ.

2 Thessalonians 3:5

True purity—got some? Want some? Not even sure what it is? Then you've come to the right place. True purity ain't what you think. In fact, it might not even be what the adults in your life think.

A Dirty Water Story

There's a common practice among well-meaning speakers that talk about purity, and it goes something like this: Take two bottles of water and set one aside. Have someone open the other bottle and drink from it. Now give it to someone else and have them drink from it. Do this five or six times, then take that backwashed bottle along with the unopened bottle and ask someone in the audience, "Which bottle would you want—the unopened, pure bottle or the one that's dirty from being passed around to who knows who? Who would want that?" This illustration and many others like it are being used to convince young people to wait to have sex before marriage. The race is on to tell you this dirty water story before you have a chance to offer your water to someone. But there are two major problems with these kinds of stories:

1. It ignores the fact that there are likely many "dirty water" people in the audience hearing the message and thinking, "Who would want me?"
2. The speaker doesn't understand, or at least doesn't accurately communicate, what purity really is or where it comes from.

What we want to do with this book is get real about what true purity is. We want to show you that it's not about how you get it or how you keep it; purity is not what you do or don't do. And here's the kicker: true purity is found in a person who isn't you and can never be you.

A Dirty Secret

When someone at your church says, "We are having a purity weekend!" what's the first thing that comes to mind? Probably dating, relationships, and sex (or the planned absence of them from your life!). While purity *does* affect how you make decisions in those areas of your life, true purity is not about saying no to you-know-what. Truth is, a lot of adults in the church use the word *purity* in a really limited sense to convey an important message on an important topic. They're not lying to you when they say that the decisions you make about your body and sex before marriage have huge implications for your physical, emotional, and spiritual life. But purity isn't about just saying no; purity (or the lack of it) affects every aspect of your life, and sex is just one of those areas. So if you limit your understanding of purity, you might just miss out on who God is, what he has done, and who you are.

You see, in order to keep you from making "the biggest mistake of your life," many adults have made sex the be-all and end-all of purity. They create purity pledges, purity balls, and purity rings. What they are really talking about is abstinence, which is something Christians and non-Christians alike can practice. They make your self-effort to remain sexually pure their number one spiritual ambition for you; how to save yourself for marriage, remain abstinent, and avoid STDs and unwanted pregnancies is worthy education, after all. But premarital sex and all its side effects are just symptoms of an impure life, not the extent of it. **Purity in the life of faith is a heart issue.** It's more about how much of yourself—your heart, mind, and soul—you have given to your passions and your desires for the things of this world than it is about just your love life. When you fail to love God with 100 percent of your heart, as Jesus taught in Matthew 22:37, your devotion to God becomes impure, tainted by a love for this world that pulls at you and drags you in the opposite direction of faith. And we *all* fail at that 100 percent thing, by the way. It's that failure, this impure devotion (or sin), that leads you to give yourself to the pursuit of happiness in the things of this world rather than in the presence of God.

When your heart is tainted by the love of this world and the pursuit of all its goodies, whether you are sexually immoral or not, you are living an impure life. Boom. Let that sink in. You are no longer living to bring God all the glory but are holding on to a little bit of that glory, or happiness, for yourself. This impurity then starts to invade all the areas of your life like an infection slowly creeps through your bloodstream and soon takes over your entire body. As you let the impurity of devoting yourself to something other than God distract your heart, steal your thoughts, and control your actions, you end up obeying the call of your flesh to do things that you desperately don't want to do but can't seem to stop. Then things start to control you. You start to say things like "I just can't help it" or "I wish I could stop." You end up going places you never meant to go and doing things you never wanted to do, and life gets out of control. You wonder why you don't feel the way you used to feel about God. You start to have pangs of guilt, feelings of loss, and aches of regret. And slowly, like the infection that infiltrates the body, the bacteria of impurity pollutes your soul and the fire you used to feel for God dims, while your passion for the things of this world is stoked. This is the essence of impurity.

When your pursuit and understanding of purity aren't about your body but are about loving the Lord your God with 100 percent of your heart, soul, mind, and strength, your focus changes. "How far is too far?" "How soon is too soon?" and "What can we do together without having actual sex?" are no longer questions in your mind or on your lips. The things that used to control you, that you used to obsess over, and that used to wreak havoc on your life are no longer "wreaking," because your life is consumed with one thing and one thing only: your love for God. This truly pure devotion, this supernatural giving of 100 percent of yourself to him, is also called holiness. When you are holy, you are separated or cut off from the unclean or impure things of this world and devoted solely to the purpose of loving and serving God. So **holiness is a good synonym for purity.** As we see in 1 Thessalonians 4:7, "God did not call us to be impure, but to live a holy life" (NIV). If you've been feeling like there is more to life, if you've experienced the fire of spiritual passion and want more of it, it's because this holiness is the call on your life. It is your purpose as a child of God, his plan for you, and his description of your future. When you give your life to Christ, he calls you away from the world to look to heaven in pursuit of higher things.

But how does it all happen? How do you become less consumed with the stuff of this world and more consumed with the God of eternity? How is living pure even possible when everyone continues to sin? Isn't this just all about willpower and self-control? If those are the thoughts going through your head right now, then you've come to the right place, because that's just what this little book is all about.

You shall

love the Lord your God

with

all your heart

and with

all your soul

and with

all your mind.

Matthew 22:37

If you love God and call yourself a believer, you naturally want more of him. If that's the condition of your heart, then good for you, because that is all that you need to start—the desire for more. That's because **your purity is really God's job.** He is the answer to your struggles with pure living. And he has made a way for you. After all, we read in Titus 2:14 that he "gave himself for us to redeem us from all lawlessness and to **purify** for himself a people for his own possession who are zealous for good works." Jesus sacrificed himself so that you could become pure, purified by his blood. This little piece of knowledge should give you a lot of peace because **this whole pure living thing isn't about you doing more, being more, or giving more but about believing that it has already been done and given.** The pure life is well within your grasp and ready for you to take hold of because of what Christ has done. We'll go into this more as we move through the book, especially in the last chapter, but for now, believe us when we say **this book isn't about your strength but his, and it isn't about your failure but his success.**

To Our Dirty Water Peeps

If you are like us, you are one of those "dirty water" people—you've gone too far sexually before marriage. Supposedly, no one wants you as much as they want the unopened bottle. Well, let us replace those lies with this truth: When God sees you, if you have accepted Christ as the Lord of your life, he sees you as pure because of Christ's shed blood and his Spirit in you. And as the Spirit works in your life, he moves you to become more and more like him, to have the mind of Christ. In other words, you don't start pure and hold on so you don't lose it; you start out as a sinner in need of Christ's purity, then are changed over time to become like him. And all the while, God sees you as pure because of his Son. Wow!

Turning on the Lights

Do you ever feel like you are walking around in the dark? When stuff happens and you are clueless what to do about it, when you do things you don't want to do, when you just can't make any progress spiritually, it can feel like the lights are off and no one is home. If only the lights were turned on and you could see what was going on around you, then you could make better decisions, understand life more, and be more prepared for the things that come at you. In John 8:12 Jesus talks about turning on the lights when he says, "I am the light of the world. Whoever follows me will not walk in darkness, but will have the light of life." In the light is where things become pure. Darkness hides all kinds of mold and disease, filth and mess. But the light disinfects; it purifies and cleanses. And as John continues the analogy in 1 John 1:7, we read that "if we walk in the light, as he is in the light, we have fellowship with one another, and the blood of Jesus his Son cleanses us from all sin." In the light, things are cleansed. This idea of light is easy to understand if you think about your life like a big house with a lot of rooms. In each room there is a light switch, but it isn't on in all of them. Some of them are well lit, like maybe the entryway, and the rooms that face the street have all the curtains open and the lights shining. But in some part of your house you might have a room or two that you keep dark—rooms you don't want anyone to see into, so you keep the lights off. In those rooms you can hide all kinds of things from prying eyes. There you can keep your secrets, your fears, your worries, and your doubts. And it is in those areas of darkness where you fail to let the light of Jesus shine in and clean up the mess.

Light on the mess can be a hard thing. It can make you feel vulnerable and weak, and it can seem easier to just avoid the light altogether. But if you want your life to be pure—if you want pure devotion, pure love, pure relationships, a pure future, and a pure faith—then you have to let the light shine onto the areas of your life you have kept in darkness. You do this through the power of Christ and the working of his Word.

Another way of thinking about light is realizing that certain types of ultraviolet light actually purify. Bacteria in water and in the air you breathe can be killed just by shining a light on it. That's what a life in the light can do.

If you've spent any time in church, you've probably heard about abiding in Christ (see John 15), and while that idea isn't always natural or obvious, it's where true purity lies. Abiding means to remain or dwell, and it is a part of living in the light. Jesus is the light, so when you live or abide in him, you live in the light. In the next chapters we are going to concentrate on how you live in Christ—what that means and how it looks in your everyday life. So get ready because we are going to turn the lights on, take the blinders off, and open up your vision to the truly pure life: a life in Christ.

If purity for you up till now has only been about sex, then you might have areas in your life where your purity has been ignored. But if you will take this journey with us, with open eyes and an open heart, you will find out what it's like to live a life 100 percent devoted to the one who is your purity. And as you do, you will see the beauty of living a pure life, unpolluted by the things that used to control you and attempted to master you. So keep reading along with us, and we will help you abide in the One who gives us our purity.

true
purity...

in love

The feeling of love can make you do some crazy things, things you said you would never do, things you never dreamed were possible. Love trumps every other feeling. Hungry, but in love? Suddenly food isn't important. Tired, but with the one you love? Who needs sleep? Content, but your love is hurting? Your heart aches for them. Love pushes its way into your heart and takes the wheel. It drives all other feelings and actions. Love is a truly powerful thing; in the pursuit of it wars are started and kingdoms fall. Love is the ultimate pursuit of the human heart, and that's why we all want it so badly that getting it or keeping it can make us do some pretty unbelievable things.

We all want love, whether we admit it or not. To love and be loved is one of the most important things in our lives, but it also can be one of the most dangerous. When you love someone, you are vulnerable. Vulnerable to rejection and pain and vulnerable to doing things you one day will regret. Love can mess with a person; it can control you, consume you, and obsess you. It can get your heart racing and your hormones raging, and in the end love can leave you with nothing but a broken heart and a guilty conscience. So how do you learn to love the way you were made to love? How do you protect your heart? How do you attain true purity in love?

Dating and Love

When it comes to the opposite sex, love can be confusing and tempting. Do you love them? Do they love you? Where will things go? Knowing what to make of your love life is an important thing. Whether you are dating or waiting, your purity will still be tested when it comes to your feelings for the opposite sex. Since love is so closely associated with feelings like excitement, lust, and other hormone-influenced stuff, being pure while you're in love can be a big challenge.

When it comes to love and dating, the most asked question is "How far is too far?" There are two reasons why you might ask yourself this. One is because you don't want to sin, so you want to know the rules that will keep you "pure" in God's eyes. That's probably the thing you are thinking about the most, but you might also ask "How far is too far?" because deep down you want to enjoy yourself, and knowing how far you can go tells you how much fun you can have without regret or guilt. Once you know how far is too far, you can let yourself go and enjoy the safety of your purity boundaries. But as you might have already figured out, once you bump into those boundaries and see how close you are to the other side of those fences, it's easy to be tempted to squeeze through the barbed wire to experience the greener pastures on the other side, and suddenly, before you know it, the boundaries have moved an inch, a foot, or maybe even a mile. Then, after it's too late, you figure out that "How far is too far?" was the wrong question.

A better question than "How far is too far?" might be "Why am I in this relationship?" Let's try that one, shall we? If you are in a relationship right now, or dreaming of one, think about your reasons for love. Why do you want this person? Why would being with them be a good thing? Before you read on, think about this question, and if you don't have a particular person you are thinking of a relationship with, then just think about relationships in general. Why do you want a relationship? What is the purpose? To be loved? To have someone to do things with? To feel good about yourself? To feel special? To find romance, sex, or entertainment? Think it over before you go on. We'll be waiting . . .

Okay. Did you do it? Did you answer the question "Why am I in this relationship?" The way you answered will help you get a good read on the purity of your heart in relationships. It's like this: If your first answer wasn't "To glorify God," then your heart isn't 100 percent purely devoted to God. If "To glorify God" was at least a part of your answer, along with some other reasons, then maybe your heart is 85 percent or even 99 percent pure. And that's normal—not pure, but normal. See, the goal of this book is to help you become pure. It's not to point fingers at you for not being perfect but to help you see those areas of impurity you may have been blind to. Why do you mess up in relationships? Why do you go too far? Because your heart is set on something other than giving God the glory. When your heart is pure, devoted to only *God's* pleasure and not your own, then staying pure in relationships is a much easier thing to do.

See, people want boundaries on their love lives so that they can be given some room to run, to kick up their heels, and to revel in the pleasures of the flesh without feelings of guilt. When you have boundaries that you or someone else have defined, you can enjoy yourself without looking over your shoulder, and that's why we all naturally want boundaries. But God doesn't give them, does he? If you look at his Word, you don't see the exact line you can go up to without sinning. There isn't a list of can-do's, like "You can hold hands, kiss on the lips, and hug as long as your hands stay above a certain line." That's because purity is not about boundaries but about the state of your heart and its devotion.

God is good. And he gave us relationships because they are good. They bring a lot of pleasure in so many ways, and that is so good. But pleasure can also be destructive when it's misunderstood, misplaced, or even abused. **So what is the purpose of your relationship—your pleasure, theirs, or God's?**

Your Pleasure

Pleasure in and of itself is not a sin. God showers us with all kinds of pleasure. He gives us food that is enjoyable to eat, sun that is fun to play in, water that feels great to float on, relationships that bring us a lot of happiness, but in all this his will is the same. As Paul puts it in his letter to the Corinthians, "'All things are lawful for me,' but not all things are helpful. 'All things are lawful for me,' but I will not be dominated by anything" (1 Cor. 6:12). This means that you can enjoy life and find pleasure in the things of this world, but not to the point that it is no longer helpful. And looking for pleasure at the expense of faithfulness, looking for pleasure in the things that God has chosen not to make holy for you, is downright harmful. When love is about you and your pleasure, you find yourself giving in to your passions, both physical and emotional, and living with regret because of it.

Let's take a look at a few ways that love goes wrong in relationships and see if we can't turn things around and help you to allow God to purify your heart and make it all about him.

Physical Love

Physical love is feeling-based. It is all about how hot they are and how hot they make you. Physical love is about you and your pleasure, about the nerves and touch receptors of your body sending signals to your brain that your brain then processes as "YAY!" In this kind of love you dream or fantasize about how good it feels to be with them. You imagine the scene; you dream of the things you'll do together. They don't even have to be sinful things—they can be sweet, romantic things—but they are ultimately all about how you feel. Or they might be a little naughty, but they are just fantasies, after all; you're never gonna actually do them, and so you feel safe. But in all these scenarios the relationship is all about you and your pleasure. While God is for your pleasure, he's for your pleasure *within his will*. And jumping into a relationship that isn't within his will—i.e., not a marriage relationship—is actually rebellion against his will. It's you saying, "God, your plans are not good enough for me. Mine are much better." It's rejecting his pace of life and opting for the fast route to pleasure.

The truth is that any kind of relationship that is based on satisfying yourself is bound to fail in some way because no one will satisfy you 100 percent of the time. Since no one is perfect (including you!), there are bound to be fights, betrayal, anger, and much more. And when love is all about your pleasure, no more pleasure means no more love.

Basing a relationship on impure love is delusional because it's based on the lie that a divided heart can be fully devoted to two separate things—devoted to serving both God and self. When your heart is divided between love for another human and love for God, you are of two minds, divided in your thinking and in your loyalty. The double-minded are unstable, according to James 1:8. And James also tells us, "Draw near to God, and he will draw near to you. Cleanse your hands, you sinners, and purify your hearts, you double-minded" (James 4:8).

In order to have pure love, you have to give God all of your heart, and we see that in the words of Jesus when he was asked what is the greatest commandment. He said, "You shall love the Lord your God with all your heart and with all your soul and with all your mind.

The Impure Waters of Love

In Ephesians 5:3 God talks about the purity of your life when he says, "But among you there must not be even a hint of sexual immorality, or of any kind of impurity, or of greed, because these are improper for God's holy people" (NIV). *Hint* is a good word here, because it speaks to anything that is less than 100 percent. Anything that has a hint of a second substance in it is no longer pure.

A hint of bacteria in your water makes the water impure. Would you want to drink water that just had a hint of poison in it? A hint could make you sick. Too much of a hint could kill you. This is how you have to think of the purity of your heart. Even a hint of the poison of self-glorification, or self-pleasure, through sex or greed or any other impurity, pollutes the waters of your heart.

This is the great and first commandment.
And a second is like it: You shall love your
neighbor as yourself" (Matt. 22:37–39).
How could Jesus say that to love God with
100 percent of ourselves and then love others
as well is the greatest fulfillment of the law?
Doesn't that math not add up? If we give 100
percent to God *plus* give love to others, doesn't
that come out to over 100 percent of ourselves
and thus divide our hearts?

It would if loving others wasn't a part of loving
God with all of ourselves. See, **in order to truly love
another, you must first love God with everything in
you.** You can't reserve some of your love in order to give
it to another. But that's exactly what you do when you love
another for the pleasure they bring you with no regard for
the love of God. In other words, when you love the physical pleasure they can give you even though that physical
pleasure is forbidden by God, or when you love how they
make you feel so much that you will ignore God's voice in
order to think of them, be with them, or work to get them
or keep them, then you are keeping a portion of your heart
from God. But true love, pure love, has as its foundation
pure devotion to God and all of his Word. When you turn
your back on any part of God's Word in order to find
love, then your love is no longer pure but tainted and
not blessed by God. This happens because you are
listening to your flesh rather than his Spirit, and

in this condition you typically find yourself in a lot of emotional and spiritual distress. Look at the words of Romans 8:5–8 on the subject:

> For those who live according to the flesh set their minds on the things of the flesh, but those who live according to the Spirit set their minds on the things of the Spirit. For to set the mind on the flesh is death, but to set the mind on the Spirit is life and peace. For the mind that is set on the flesh is hostile to God, for it does not submit to God's law; indeed, it cannot. Those who are in the flesh cannot please God.

This is the danger with a divided heart. True love first requires pure devotion—not to the people of this earth but to the God of heaven.

Idol Love

Another sure sign of impure love is your love for idols: the dream of the unattainable affection of a movie star or singer. When Hayley was young she had posters of her favorite singers all over her walls. In fact, she loved one boy so much that she got into a fight with her best friend over who would marry him. The friendship almost ended, but then Hayley agreed that the other girl could have him (or at least his poster exclusivity). Of course, the girl never even met him, but this kind of hopeful love can easily feed your fantasies and keep you in a kind of worshipful stupor that drives you to evangelize others into the love of your idols, to talk about them incessantly, and to do all you can to study them and to learn more about them. This devotion then takes a huge chunk of your heart, pulling you away from your passion for your first love, God himself (see Rev. 2:4).

Nonbelieving Love

There is another kind of impure love that very few people want to know about, let alone talk about, and that is dating a nonbeliever. When you fall in love with someone who doesn't love God, you are making a choice to reach for your own pleasure over God's glory. What makes us say this? Check out 2 Corinthians 6:14–16:

Do not be unequally yoked with unbelievers. For what partnership has righteousness with lawlessness? Or what fellowship has light with darkness? What accord has Christ with Belial? Or what portion does a believer share with an unbeliever? What agreement has the temple of God with idols?

This means that **God doesn't want his children to partner with, or to fall in love with and marry, nonbelievers.** That is because nonbelievers live in darkness, and believers live in the light. As 1 John 1:5–6 says, "God is light, and in him is no darkness at all. If we say we have fellowship with him while we walk in darkness, we lie and do not practice the truth." When you date someone who is walking in darkness, as are all non-believers, you spend a bunch of your time walking with them, and so you walk in darkness too (see Prov. 13:20; 1 Cor. 15:33; 2 Cor. 4:4; Eph. 5:11). And in the dark you find impure love, not the pure love meant for the children of God (see 1 John 1:6–7).

It can be hard to walk away from the romantic love you feel for a nonbeliever, but as a child of God you've gotta make the choice. Will you defy God and love him with only a portion of your heart so that you can partner with an unbeliever in love? Or will you defy the romantic love that you feel in favor of loving God with all your heart, soul, and mind? Remember that **to love God with only a portion of your heart so that you can defy him with another portion is a recipe for the spiritual disaster of impure love.**

Their Pleasure

When the purpose of the love in your life is your pleasure, it's all about you, and God takes a backseat. But what about when your purpose in love is *their* pleasure— the pleasure of the one you love? Surely that's biblical and pure love. Surely there's nothing wrong with that. After all, Philippians 2:3 says that we are

Can Nonbelievers Love?

We love because and only because God first loved us (see 1 John 4:19). His love for us and his Holy Spirit living inside of us give us the ability to love the way God loves. This kind of love then centers on the will and the desire of God, not of people. So the question then pops up: **Can a nonbeliever love at all?** After all, they don't have the Holy Spirit, so what about their love? Well, good thing you asked. Some might say that some nonbelievers even love better than Christians. They can be compassionate, giving, and caring. Many of them actively look for ways to improve the world. And that's all true, many nonbelievers love, but the real question isn't what do they do but *why do they do it*. Motive has a lot to do with the purity of love. For the nonbeliever, of course, the motive in love isn't bringing glory to God but to themselves. The nonbeliever loves, ultimately, because of what it does for them. It makes them feel good, important, loved, free from guilt, that they are leaving a legacy, and the list goes on. The person who doesn't love God cannot know true love because true love comes from God. In 1 John 4:16 we see that God is love, and therefore a person must abide in God in order to have true love in their lives.

Christian love is a deeper and more significant thing because its motive isn't self-serving but selfless. Like the love Jesus showed for us by taking on human form, coming to earth, and dying on that cross, true love isn't about self in any way, shape, or form but is about the Father and his love for us. So if you are God's kid, his love runs in your blood. He is your Father and your role model; that's why Ephesians 5:1–2 says that we are to "be imitators of God, as beloved children. And walk in love, as Christ loved us and gave himself up for us, a fragrant offering and sacrifice to God." We can love a pure love because "God's love has been poured into our hearts through the Holy Spirit who has been given to us" (Rom. 5:5). Love defines the believer.

When the Holy Spirit starts to convict you about your relationship, consider it a red flag waving over a sign that says, "How much of your heart does God get?" If your answer is less than 100 percent, then you've gotta reassess your definition of love to include giving him all your heart, soul, mind, and strength and out of that dedication loving others the way he loved you—selflessly.

to consider others better than ourselves, doesn't it? It sure does. So does that mean that staying pure in love means giving your loved one pleasure? Sounds logical, doesn't it? There is some trouble in that logic, though. The trouble is that it gives more importance to a person's pleasure than to God's. When we do that, everything gets out of whack. See, pleasure isn't always pure. In fact, a lot of the time it's downright impure. So to say that in order to love someone I have to give them pleasure (or another way of putting it is "always make them happy") is an impure way of thinking. **God's goal isn't to make everyone happy but is to make us holy. Our goal in life should be similar—not our happiness but our holiness.**

Conditional

Love becomes impure when it's conditional. "I'll love you if you _____" or even "If you loved me you would _____" reveals the conditions of their love. Essentially this statement means, "If you do this for me, then I'll know you love me, and so I will love you back, or at least pretend to." See the condition? I need to get this first before I'll give you love in return. That is not love! Love doesn't make demands, ever! Love doesn't hold goodness, kindness, gentleness, patience, or anything good back until its demands are met or until love is proven. True love is never conditional, so no one can put conditions on you like saying, "Do this or you don't love me."

What ultimately happens when you give in to the conditions of love and do what your loved one asks so that they will love you back is that you make love all about you. Sure, it seems like it's all about them and their "needs," but ultimately it comes down to you and your need to be loved. It's a selfish love you give when you give it in order to get something back. That's not love. Pure love is never about getting but always about giving. It never has ulterior motives, giving in order to get, but gives whether anything is given in return or not. If your motive for giving yourself to someone is to get something in return, then you are not in a pure love relationship but in an impure one.

Keeping the Peace

Another impurity can enter love when we do things with the motive of keeping the peace. It goes something like this. The one you love is emotional, and when they don't get their way or they are hurt by something someone says or does, there is going to be drama. They are going to blow up or withdraw. They are going to take it out on you in some way or another, so you do whatever they ask in order to keep the peace. That seems to make sense since God is a God of peace—he wants you to look for ways to make peace, he wants you to serve others, to care for them, and to make their lives comfortable, right? Well, that sure sounds biblical, but is it? Not exactly. See, God isn't all about your comfort but your purity. He isn't about your happiness but your righteousness, and so **he isn't glorified or pleased when the comfort of another takes first place in your life.**

For example, say you have a girlfriend or boyfriend who is going to lose it if you don't go along with their bitterness. If they are raging about something someone did to them and are all up in arms about it and want you to join them in their rant, you can refuse to join in, but look out, because then they'll be just as mad at you. In this example, keeping the peace involves you joining in the insanity of their bitter, gossipy, angry sin. And that's putting them and their will above God and his. Get the picture? **Whenever someone wants you to join them in their sin, to encourage their sin, or even to overlook their sin and just keep your mouth shut to make them happy, they are demanding impurity in your life.** They are asking you to love God with less of your heart so that you can love them and their sin with a little portion, if not all of it. And this is an impure love.

In these situations the answer is pure love, and that is a love that is first of all kind, patient, and self-controlled, filled with the fruit of the Spirit (see Gal. 5:22–23) but also unwilling to sin in order to keep

Hayley's Impure Love

Once upon a time I fell in love with a nonbeliever. Knowing that God didn't want me to be unequally yoked, I still slipped and allowed myself to fall very hard for this guy. Once I realized I couldn't change him and that we could never be together, I broke things off, but it was the hardest thing I'd ever done. To defy the feelings of romantic love is painful, and it gets more painful the longer you put it off. If you are in love with someone who doesn't love God, then walk away while you can—before you find yourself living with an impure love that will break your heart.

someone happy. And pure love is fearless in the insistence that God is good and his Word is useful for teaching, correcting, and pointing out error (see 2 Tim. 3:16). To remain pure you must not give in to the whims of other people but must insist on letting the love of God be your guide.

Giving Love to Get Love

Love doesn't respond with either conditions or selfishness. And **giving anything, including love, in order to get love, to be loved, to feel loved is impure love.** When love has to do with how you feel, you are gonna find yourself giving things in order to get that feeling of love in your life. But in order to stay 100 percent pure for God and not for yourself, you can't confuse feelings with love. Certainly **love can be an amazing feeling, but amazing feelings aren't always love.** If your goal is to give someone love, to focus on them, then ask yourself why. Why do I want to love them so much? Why do I want to give them all they ask, all they desire, all they want? What is my goal? If it is to get them to do the same for you, or even just to get them to love you, then your love is impure, tainted with the stain of selfishness, and it is not love at all but self-obsession. And this self-obsessed kind of love is weak, fed only on the whims of broken and unrighteous humanity (see Rom. 3:10), and this is a weak foundation.

Accepting Violence

God wants all of us to love others, but when love turns either physically violent or psychologically abusive, some accept the violence because they love and fear their abuser more than they love and fear God. In this way of thinking, the victim is so obsessed with their abuser—so obsessed with either keeping them happy or not risking a breakup—that they stay in the abusive relationship. This might look like humility gone wrong, but it's really a warped form of pride. That's because pride is all about making self look good, and the victim of abuse wants so badly to be seen as lovable by their abuser that they will accept any-thing if it means they might one day be loved more. Still others just fear what people might think so much that they won't get out of the relationship for fear of losing face. In both situations it's all about the pleasure of others, with the ironic motive of self-protection. All of this is just pride in sheep's clothing.

You must know that there is no room for vio-lence in love (see Matt. 5:21–22; James 1:19–20). Selfless love isn't consumed with another human being but with God. Its goal isn't the pleasure of man but of God. If you want to be pure in your love relationships, then protect the temple of God, your body, and don't allow others to use you for their own sinful purposes.

You can't love others with a pure love when you fail to love God with your all. Allowing the one you love to become more important than God by giving in to their sinful choices pollutes your love relationship. Perfect love is found in the life of God in you, in acting in accordance with his Holy Spirit, not on the whims of others.

God's Pleasure

All of us have a choice to make in relationship to others: we can love them either for our pleasure, for their pleasure, or for God's pleasure. In the search for purity in love, we have to choose the latter, God's pleasure. There is nothing pure in a love that exists outside of that goal. God's pleasure is the continual focus of the pure. As we read in 1 Corinthians 10:31, "Whether you eat or drink, or whatever you do, do all to the glory of God." The purpose of your life, as a follower of Christ, is to bring glory to God. And your relationship is a part of that purpose. It isn't meant for your joy, happiness, or fun alone, but for God's glory. So in wanting to remain 100 percent pure for God, you must ask yourself some important questions. The most important one is "Is this relationship bringing God glory?" In other words, does it serve him? Does it please him? Is it making it easier for me to live out my purpose, to minister to the world, to grow spiritually, or to love others? The purpose of your relationship is God's glory. Is it living up to that purpose? If not, then it is an impure relationship.

"How far is too far?" is the most asked question in relationships because we all realize that sexual immorality is a spiritual issue. As believers who love God and want to please him, we are naturally concerned about our physical life, as well we should be. Like every other area of our lives, our bodies are meant not for our pleasure but as a temple for his worship. You can figure this out from reading 1 Corinthians 6:20, which reminds you that "You were bought with a price. So glorify God in your body." This makes it pretty clear that your body wasn't meant to be a plaything, something you use just to get your kicks, but for a far greater purpose completely. The gifts of your body, your life, and your relationships must ultimately direct others to Christ—to his beauty, to his glory, to his power, and to his majesty. You can't do that by using your body for your own sexual pleasure in any relationship outside of marriage itself (see Eph. 5:3).

When your purity is based on who you are and what you do or don't do, it's not true purity. Whether you think that you are pure because you don't go all the way, or because you are not going to kiss until you get married, **no matter how you define your purity, if it's based on what you do instead of what Christ has done,**

it's not purity at all but a cheap imitation of purity, a human attempt to do the work of the Savior. For Hayley, this attempt to be pure by herself actually led her away from God when she decided she just wasn't good enough for him. For Michael, his pursuit of purity left him nursing along sinful relation-ships in order to do the "honorable" thing. These are just two examples of how concentrating the pursuit of purity on how good you are, how far you go, or how to purify your mess-ups can be a tragic thing. We don't want this book to be a how-to manual or a list of dos and don'ts that will keep you on the "good person" list. What we want to do is to talk to you about pure faith and how it reveals itself in pure love and so affects all your love relationships.

Your Family

Community is important to God; he lives in it, and he gave you your family so that you could live in it as well. Community is essential to the life of faith. You can't bring glory to God while living in isolation, but God's glory comes through you showing his love to those around you.

Since your family is usually such a close community, it's one of the first places where impurity can rear its ugly head. When you don't love your family, when you argue, resent, despise, or reject your family, you

Hayley's Fear of Hell

When I was in high school, I thought impurity would keep me out of heaven (and send me to hell). So I did everything I could to stay pure. No matter what, I would save myself for marriage because I didn't want to make God mad or to lose my place in heaven. I also was scared to death of getting pregnant, and after sitting through health class, I sure didn't want to get an STD. So out of fear I kept myself pure. Or at least as pure as I could.

After working so hard to control myself, to avoid losing my virginity or catching anything from anybody, I started to wear down. Over time the strength left me, and I just couldn't keep up self-control. I started to slip and to slide, and before I knew it I wasn't as pure as I always intended to be. I decided that my mess-ups were too much to qualify me for heaven, and so I gave up on being good, gave up on trying to stay pure, and just gave in to the temptations to do the things I had always said I wouldn't do. And as a result, I was sure that God had given up on me because I hadn't kept my purity.

reject the very Word of God that clearly calls you to love. Jesus explained this when he said, "A new commandment I give to you, that you love one another: just as I have loved you, you also are to love one another. By this all people will know that you are my disciples, if you have love for one another" (John 13:34–35). When your love for your family is impure, tainted by sin, you no longer look like a disciple of Christ but act like a child of this world. And your ultimate familial relationship, the one with your holy Father, suffers. That's why in any discussion of purity, it is essential that we talk about the family relationship. Let's take a look at pure love for your parents and siblings.

Loving Your Parents

When you think of purity you probably most often think of a boy with a girl. But dating isn't the only area where impurity is a problem. Loving those who are closest to you can be one of the most challenging things. It's been said a million times, but let's say it again in case you weren't listening: God wants you to "honor your father and your mother" (Exod. 20:12). That means that in order to love God with your all, you must love your parents by showing them honor in everything you do. But that can be easier said than done. Your parents don't do everything right— really, sometimes they don't seem to do anything

Michael's Plans for Marriage

When I was growing up, my parents told me amazing stories about their great romantic love affair. I was the youngest of six kids, and they were married for forty-seven years before my dad died. My dad never talked about any old girlfriends or about being a ladies' man, only about his long and undying love for my mother. The only problem with that was, I thought that once I fell in love with someone, I was going to marry them. Since I never felt like that about anyone in high school, waiting for "the one" was easy. But then I met her. And I was sure I would marry her. So I had sex with her. Then we broke up. This process would repeat and repeat, and all the while I was looking to marriage to restore my "purity," to redeem my past mistakes, which made me stay in relationships I would've broken off if I hadn't felt so guilty. For me, purity wasn't so much about what I did or didn't do with my body but about having a pure intent—I wanted to marry every girl I was with physically. Until eventually I didn't.

right! How can you honor them when they are so messed up? Well, it's easier than you might think, because the answer has less to do with your parents and more to do with God.

See, when God commands something, he doesn't command it based on our actions or response but on his. Let's explain. God commands you to obey authority (see Heb. 13:17). This command doesn't say anything about whether or not you agree with that authority. It simply relies on your love for and obedience to God. And the same is true for honoring parents. Your call is to glorify God by honoring your parents, not to honor your parents by obeying God. God is the originator of this relationship, and he is the one who set it up so that glorifying God will lead you to honor your father and mother.

In other words, it isn't about who your parents are, what they do, or how they act, but it's about who God is and what he has asked you to do. It's like your relationship with the traffic cop who pulls you over. You don't have to agree with his religion, his values, or his way of life, but you do have to obey his commands to stay in the car, keep your hands where he can see them, and give him your license. You do this because you respect the position of police officer, not necessarily the man himself. The same is true for messed-up parents. You might not agree with everything they do, but that is irrelevant in the life of purity. What is relevant is honoring God with your life by honoring the people he has set up for you to honor here on earth.

But what does this honor look like? How do you act with your parents so that God gets all the glory? Well, the first place we should always look is to the list of fruit we saw earlier in Galatians 5:22–23. This list of things that come from the Spirit of God tells us the things that bring him glory by revealing his nature to the world, and so this list is foundational to all pure relationships. Let's take a look so you can think about how they relate to your relationship with your parents:

Love

Joy

Peace

Patience

Kindness

Goodness

Faithfulness

Gentleness

Self-control

Pure love involves reacting to the difficult situations in your life with these charac- teristics. When things are good at home and your parents are doing everything you want them to do, these reactions aren't hard to muster. But when things get tough and emotions flare, the opposite of these are more likely to show up. We call these **the fruit of the flesh**, and they are:

Selfishness

Joylessness

Conflict

Impatience

Mercilessness

Sinfulness

Unfaithfulness

Pride

Self-indulgence

If any of these things show up in your relationship with your parents, then impurity has seeped into your life in the form of the fruit of the flesh. Have you ever considered that God put your parents in your life not just to teach you about growing up and being good but to give you the opportunity to rely on the Holy Spirit to inform your decisions, to guide you, and to shape you into the likeness of Christ? After all, without trials and testing, you don't grow. And sometimes some of the biggest testing takes place at home.

When it comes to your family, you need to call on the Holy Spirit and allow him to speak to you and guide you into the kind of honor that brings glory to God.

When your flesh screams for self-indulgence or conflict, his Spirit whispers for self-control and peace. And
while the fruit of the Spirit don't come naturally to you,
his Spirit can guide you and teach you supernaturally so
that you can do what people without the Spirit can't: honor
your parents with a pure honor that comes from a heart of
selflessness rather than a heart of selfishness.

If there is conflict in your home, take some time to think
about the situations when it happens and your reactions
to your parents, and then look at the list of the fruit of the
flesh. See if any of them are involved in your behavior or
thoughts. If they are, then quit blaming your miserable
problems on your parents instead of your own impurity. If
you ignore the Holy Spirit when your temper flares, you
are just rejecting God in favor of your flesh and purity in
favor of poison. "For if you live according to the flesh
you will die, but if by the Spirit you put to death the
deeds of the body, you will live" (Rom. 8:13).

Every relationship God allows in your life offers
the chance for his Spirit to show itself. When you
interact with your parents in pure love, you act
not in the flesh but in the Spirit, and when
that happens things go much better for you.
Your parents might not become what you
want them to be. Since they are sinners,
just like you, it should be no surprise
when they sin. If and when they let you
down (just like you have probably let

them down at some point), remember that your Father in heaven will never fail you. He'll never fall and never sin, so he can always be trusted. As long as your parents aren't asking you to sin, honor God and give him the glory by honoring your parents.

Loving Your Brothers and Sisters

As a part of your community, God may also have given you siblings. They just offer another opportunity for you to remember Christ is your purity. Sometimes the most difficult people to be nice to are your own flesh and blood, and this is especially true of siblings, but the same applies to your relationship with them as with your parents: God is glorified when you show them the fruit of the Spirit. He even says as much in Psalm 133:1: "How good and pleasant it is when brothers dwell in unity!" This unity displays that you are children of God. It displays your honor and your respect for the Father by revealing your ability to die to yourself and your own needs in order to serve and to love the people who test you the most.

An important thing to understand about the fruit of the Spirit as it reveals itself in your family is that this fruit is meant to feed others. Think about a fruit tree. It grows apples, oranges, or some other kind of fruit for the people who would come and eat from it. The fruit tree doesn't consume the fruit itself (except maybe through decomposition as the fruit falls from the limbs and slowly nourishes the soil where the tree is planted). The fruit that grows on the limbs and reaches out to the world is meant to feed others. The same is true with the fruit of the Spirit—your joy, your self-control, your peace is meant to nourish your brothers and sisters in the love of God. That's why it's so important to act in the Spirit and not in the flesh when you are with them. It's important to be a beacon pointing the way to the Father for those who see you every day. Impurity invades your life when you reject the voice of the Holy Spirit urging you to love your family and instead choose to attack, to hate, or to divide.

If you are lacking purity in your life, and if you feel distant from God and empty, the first place to look is at home. Your relationship with your family sets the tone for your whole life and reveals the depths you will go to glorify God with your life. Are you willing to give him the glory and to reject your desire to be right, to be bitter, to be unkind? If you are, then purity will define you and your relationships will change. But if you are unwilling to practice purity at home, then impurity will color every aspect of your life. You can't be impure at home and pure in the world; you are either living in the purity of Christ or you are not. Don't let impurity seep into your life through the safety of your own four walls. But make your family the place where purity starts and grows stronger so that you can maintain it in every area of your life.

As a lover of God you must remember what pleases him and bring him the glory. But how do you know what pleases God in your relationships? The answer is partially found in Colossians 1:10, which says that we are to "walk in a manner worthy of the Lord, fully pleasing to him, bearing fruit in every good work and increasing in the knowledge of God." This means that what pleases God is the growth of fruit and knowledge in your life. Fruit is the evidence of the life of the Spirit living inside of you. It is the stuff seen in Galatians 5:22–23: "But the fruit of the Spirit is love, joy, peace, patience, kindness, goodness, faithfulness, gentleness, self-control." In a pure relationship these things will grow in you, not shrink. And in 1 Corinthians 13 pure love is described like this: "Love is patient and kind; love does not envy or boast; it is not arrogant or rude. It does not insist on its own way; it is not irritable or resentful; it does not rejoice at wrongdoing, but rejoices with the truth" (vv. 4–6). Can you love with a pure love—one that doesn't just "put God first" but makes God your *all*? If God isn't all, then he isn't anything, because God must be everything to you or he isn't your master. We all serve something; whether it's God or self is up to you. But if you want true purity in love, then the power comes not from commitment rings or promises but from a heart devoted 100 percent to God through a relationship with Jesus. It means fearlessly loving him when others would run. And it means being devoted not to the voice of the flesh but to the voice of the Spirit, who speaks nothing but truth and wants nothing but a pure love that gives him everything so that you may love the world with that same kind of pure love.

true
purity...

in community

*T*he best friend in the world is the friend who loves God more than they love you. That's because when they love him, then they are able to truly love you. Are you a good friend? How's your social life? Do people flock to you or avoid you? Your social life really has less to do with who you are and more to do with who God is. When your social life is pure, you are easy to be around. But if your social life is suffering, it might just be because your heart is divided rather than purely devoted to and focused on the One who can make it all come together.

Relationships can be tough. You might have a few friends or no friends. You might even have more enemies than friends, but you have to know that friendship is important to God, and so are strangers. Relationships matter to him, and that's good news. It means that he is here to help you with all your friendship issues.

Don't believe us? Check this out. **God is a God of community: Father, Son, and Holy Spirit, three living as one.** In the beginning of the world, God created one thing after another and saw that it was good. Good, good, good! Then he found something that wasn't good, and that was isolation. It says so right in Genesis 2:18: "Then the Lord God said, 'It is not good that the man should be alone; I will make him a helper fit for him.'" See? It was not good for man to be alone because man, made in the image of God, needs others, and not just animals but other like-minded creatures made in the image of God. So in the pursuit of true purity, the area of your social life is of great importance and significance to God.

But it is in relationship with other human beings where some of your biggest problems can happen. Maybe that's why God talks about relationships so much in his Word. Yep, God has a lot to say about living in community. In fact, much of the book of wisdom called Proverbs is about the tongue and how your words either build up or tear down. And most of the New Testament is about living with other humans, encouraging and correcting our relationships. Because of that we are not at a loss to see what pure relationships are like.

Since we've already covered dating and familial relationships in the love chapter, let's take a look now at the relationships you have with **friends, enemies, and strangers** and see how you can stay pure when dealing with the up-and-down nature of living in community.

Friends

Friends are essential to the life of the believer. We were made to live with them (see Rom. 12:16), encourage them (see 1 Thess. 5:11), help them (see 1 Cor. 12:25; Phil. 2:4) and pray for them (see James 5:16). Friends remind us of who God is and who we are (see Col. 3:16). They work with us and play with us. They make our lives more bearable and more fun. Yeah, friends are great. But what kind of friendships does God want in your life? Could your friendships be impure? And if they are, how do you go from dirty to clean, impure to purified, so the friendships can be saved?

The Purpose of Friends

Friendship is meant to draw you closer to God. It should keep you on track and give you encouragement and guidance, hope and peace (see 1 Thess. 5:11). Friendship, like dating, is meant not just for entertainment or pleasure but for the purpose of bringing glory to God (see John 13:34–35). That means that true friendship is the kind that drives you closer to him (see Prov. 13:20). It helps you serve him more fully. It teaches you and sustains you in the hard times. Good friends act as the hands and feet of God to each other and provide healing (see James 5:16). And pure friendships reveal the love of God to the world that looks on (John 13:35).

Three Categories of Friends

The way we see it, friends fall into three categories, and putting your friends in their right categories is super important in keeping those friendships pure. As you read the three categories, think about your closest friends and which number they fit under:

1. Friends who are *more* spiritual than you
2. Friends who are *less* spiritual than you
3. Friends who are *about the same* as you spiritually

Friends in categories #1 and #3 are meant to influence you to purity, while you are meant to influence #2. In other words, the goal for you as a believer is to be always progressing in purity, not regressing. That means that **the only friends who should have an influence over you are the ones who are at least as faithful as you are, if not more.** Those who are less spiritual should be learning from you, not teaching you, because after all, you have more to teach in the way of truth than someone who knows less about God than you do, right?

Knowing which friends are which will help you drive your relationships toward true purity. But thinking like this means you are gonna have to change the way you act around some of your friends. Chances are you have friends who are less spiritual than you, as you should. These are the people God has given you to influence, to teach, and to encourage in the way of faith. They are the ones you are meant to invest in, in order to lead them closer to God. But if they are doing most of the leading, or even a hint of the leading, then you are making friendship more important than God. James 4:4 warns against that mistake when it says, "Whoever wishes to be a friend of the world makes himself an enemy of God." **Friendship is meant to glorify God** by being a reminder of him, a tool for him, and a witness of him. So in the area of influence, all of it is meant to come from the most spiritual person in the room, not the least. If that's you, then you should be the strongest influence in the relationship. Think about those people in your life who are less spiritual than you, maybe even don't believe in God at all. Who leads the relationship? Who has the most say? The most sway? Who counsels who? Who comforts who? Who gives who advice? If it isn't you who has the most peace, the most advice, the most joy, the most self-control, the most influence, then things are mixed up and not pure.

Now, you might have a friend who isn't the best person in the world, and you might think that just hanging out with you will help them. "After all," you think, "my good can rub off on them and teach them how great it is to be good." But according to God's Word, that isn't exactly the way things work. It's actually the other way around. First Corinthians 15:33 says, "Do not be misled: 'Bad company corrupts good character'" (NIV). A lot of people think it's the other way around—that good character changes bad character. But the bad influence is more dominant than the good. **The idea that by hanging out with the "bad influence" you can somehow "show them the light" without talking about the things of God is a broken idea, especially for those of you young in your faith.** According to God's Word, it's the good character that's going to be influenced the most. Unless you see that your influence over the weaker person is secure, such as if they are coming to you for guidance and advice and you are steering them repeatedly to God and his Word, chances are you are being more influenced by bad than they are by good.

Just like there is a problem with so-called missionary dating, there is a problem with being good friends with people who want nothing to do with God. And the problem is that they get you off course. They encourage distance from God, not intimacy with him. They feed your sinful thoughts. They fuel the fire of gossip, anger, bitterness, lust, revenge, deception, and a lot more. And they don't encourage your purity.

But how does influence take place? In what ways are you influenced by your friends? Let's take a look and see how impurity spills into relationships and how to return your friendships to purity by changing the dynamic of influence.

Advice

When someone has influence over you, you give them a say in your life. That means that when you have struggles, questions, doubts, and fears, you go to them for their opinions, their guidance, and their encouragement. If you are going to a friend who is less spiritual than you for these things, you are opening yourself up for ungodly advice that will only hurt you and not help you.

Another problem is that when you go to the weaker person for advice, you share things with them that they aren't capable of understanding. For example, your sin. They might not be prepared to understand how you keep struggling with sin when you claim to be a believer. Without a good understanding of grace, the weaker person might think that your faith is fake, hypocritical, or just plain stupid. **When you bring problems to a friend who is less spiritual than you, you expose them to things they aren't spiritually prepared to handle.** Like the parent who tells their six-year-old all about their financial problems and asks them for their input, you run the risk of confusing them, if not scaring them off, by showing your lack of strength and faith.

Advice should be sought from spiritually stronger people. After all, you want godly advice, right? So why go to the ungodly, or less godly, for things they are incapable of giving?

Agreement

Friends are people who have something in common. They agree on things, usually a lot of things, and that's why they like each other. In fact, the more time you spend with someone, the more you become like each other. Have you ever seen two friends who spend so much time together that they start dressing like each other and talking like each other? It's part of agreement. When two people who like each other spend time together, they start to agree on more and more. The Bible backs this up. Amos 3:3 says, "Can two people walk together without agreeing on the direction?" (NLT). Friends walk together because they both agree on where they are going. But should you agree on a direction with someone who isn't headed toward God? Should you allow this person to influence your path, your choices, your actions?

While you can be friends with people with less faith than you, to let them lead you is to let yourself turn away from God in order to follow the things of this world. The Spirit in you should be the main influence in your direction, not people. And someone who has less of the Spirit, or none of it, should not be part of choosing the direction or action you take.

Comfort

You need comfort from time to time. You get hurt; you fall down; you need someone to brush you off and get you back on your way. But those people who comfort you the best have influence over you. After all, their words of encouragement are what give you relief. And if their words are not pointing you toward God, then they are distracting you and polluting your life. Just like with giving advice, these spiritually weaker people are not equipped to comfort you, and you run the risk of doubting the God of comfort when you go to a friend for something that God promises to give you (see 2 Cor. 1:3).

Encouragement

Encouragement is influence, because encouragement persuades you to action, either physical, mental, or emotional. When your friends encourage you, it gives you the strength to act. That can be great, except when the encouragement is in the direction of faithlessness rather than faithfulness. For example, your friend might encourage you to go on a spring break trip with them rather than a mission trip with your church. Or they might encourage you to lie to your parents so you can spend the

night or go somewhere you shouldn't. The people who
encourage you to do things are influencing you and
guiding you, and if they are not godly people, then their
guidance isn't encouraging purity in your life.

Best Friends

Best friends influence one another more than any other
friends. Best friends are so connected, so involved with
each other that they influence almost everything in each
other's lives. That's why being best friends with someone
less spiritual than you is impure. A best friend is one you
can confide in and go to for advice, comfort, encouragement, and hope. A best friend steers your life with you;
they impact your way of thinking and of acting. Because
of their great influence over your life, **if you are a believer, you can't be best friends with a nonbeliever.**
It is another way of being unequally yoked (see 2 Cor.
6:14–16), and it is a dangerous relationship. A best
friend is meant to bring godly encouragement,
direction, and hope. They are meant to build you
up in your faith, not distract you from it.

If your life is bent on serving, loving, and
glorifying God, then anyone who doesn't
believe in God is gonna get tired of you.
They will be sick of all your God-talk.
They won't want to support God's call in
your life. They will think its weird how
you pray and "hear" from God. They

will encourage distraction and ungodly ways of thinking. **They won't encourage faithfulness, abstinence, self-control, righteousness, worship, or the essential act of dying to self and living for God.** They can't because they have no part in any of it. And if your devotion to God is deep, if you are sold out to him, then they will not understand you. When that happens you have two choices: you either change to fit their personality, or you distance yourself from them. You cannot be completely devoted to God and remain best friends with someone who rejects him.

If your bff is a nonbeliever, you might be freaking out right now, and that's okay. It's to be expected. Your eyes are being opened and you don't like what you are seeing. Conviction is doing its work. So what do you do now? Well, you gotta start with God. Talk to him; confess the areas where you have made friendship with the world more important than him. Search his Word for the purpose of friendship. Turn away (repent) from the status quo and make a change. In other words, you are going to have to back off from your best friend. You don't have to never talk to them again, but a change in the relationship is due.

Think about how you can influence them more than they influence you. See your nonbelieving friends as a mission field now. Start to pray for them, talk to them about God, share your faith more with them,

Michael's
Impure Social Life

I call myself a friendly hermit. I am good with people. I like being with them, but I prefer to be alone. Community doesn't come naturally to me. That might be because of the way I was raised. When I was a kid my parents never had anyone over, ever. My mom was too embarrassed to let anyone see our house, so we kept contact with the outside world to a minimum. I have very few memories of parties, dinners with other families, or any social time at our house. While I was the class clown at school, entertaining everyone, when I got home the socializing stopped. Hermit mode, engage. I'm still the same on the inside, but now I'm more intentional about spending time with others because I know it gives God glory when I'm helping others and letting others help me.

and explain to them how you are going deeper with God. Don't judge them, condemn them, accuse them, or even explain all this stuff to them. Just talk to them about God, about his love for you and them, about his amazingness. Become an evangelist more than a bff. If they start to freak out because of your deeper devotion, it's just confirmation that a believer cannot be best friends with a nonbeliever. Let happen what will happen. But you have to choose who you're gonna serve—yourself or your God, your best friend or your Father.

A friend can change your life. They can lead you down the wide path or the narrow path; they can encourage your faith or discourage it. Friendship matters to God, and friendship can help you to either a life of purity or a life of impurity. Don't just let friendship happen, but invite God into your relationships. Find out how you can make him happy and give him the glory in every one of your relationships, and all your friendships will be pure.

Believing Friends

Proverbs 1:7 says something foundational to faith: "The fear of the Lord is the beginning of knowledge; fools despise wisdom and instruction." In the first half of this verse we see that without the fear of the Lord, wisdom is impossible. In the second half we see that fools turn their backs on the wisdom and instruction of

God, and therefore on God himself. Knowing this, now take a look at Proverbs 13:20: "Walk with the wise and become wise, for a companion of fools suffers harm" (NIV). Who are the wise? According to Proverbs 1:7 they are those who fear the Lord, or believers. So God's command on your life is to walk with believers, and his warning is that those without wisdom, i.e., "fools," will be your downfall or lead to harm.

Pure best-friendship is friendship between two believers, and so understandably it is the subject of much of God's Word. The most common expression used to describe the friendship of believers is the term "one another." These two words are used all over the place to describe the things that believing friends do for each other. The "one anothers" are a great place to look when you want to learn more about purity in your friendships.

Friendship is so important to God. In fact, Jesus explained in John 13:35 that friendship between believers will prove our friendship with him to the rest of the world: "By this all people will know that you are my disciples, if you have **love for one another**." But what does it mean to love one another? How do we love the way God wants us to love? We can find the answer to this by looking at the other "one anothers" peppered throughout Scripture.

We are called to pray for one another (see James 5:16), encourage one another (see 1 Thess. 5:11), live in peace with one another (see Rom. 12:16), accept one another (see Rom. 14:13), comfort one another (see 2 Cor. 1:3–4), serve one another (see Gal. 5:13), bear one another's burdens (see Gal. 6:2), forgive one another (see Eph. 4:32), confess to one another (see James 5:16), and spend time with one another (see Heb. 10:25). The descriptions of the things that believers do for one another go both ways, and that's why the expression "one another" is used. If it could go just one way then it would say to do it *to* or *for* others, but "one another" means that both people comfort, confess, pray, and so on. It has to go both ways. That means that in order to apply these commands to friendship, we have to be talking about friendship between two believers. And in believing best-friendships these "one anothers" are practiced regularly.

Impure Friendships

Unfortunately, there are a lot of times when friendships get messy. They can even get polluted and toxic. When this happens, the impurity seeps into your life and floods every aspect of it. For example, when your friend turns mean and acts more like an enemy than a friend, you can find yourself with impure thoughts about them, about others, or even about yourself. What your friends do to you or what you do because of them can lead to all kinds of impure stuff. So let's take a quick look at some of the red flags of friendship that are meant to show you where impurity is seeping into your life.

Addictive Love

Friendship can be addictive, but if you are starting to feel that you are literally addicted to your friend (or friends) then your friendship is no longer pure. That's because being addicted is a synonym for idolatry—the worship of someone or something other than God. When you are addicted to someone, you become dependent on them. You need them in order to be happy, to feel safe, to be content. You think about them all the time; you want their approval, advice, and counsel more than anything else; and because of that you will do anything for them—even disobey God.

If you are addicted to your friend, you are struggling with impurity and you are losing. The only person who deserves your worship or addiction is God himself. And to allow your heart to be devoted to a human being the way you were designed to be devoted to God is a dangerous choice. If you are addicted to another human being, then the Holy Spirit will ask you to make a choice. Who will be your God? You can't have two—you can't worship another human being and God at the same time.

If this is making your heart race and your mouth dry, then be thankful that God is doing his work in you. If you want to choose him over another, then listen to the voice of God whispering in your ear and take this awakening as a call to return to him. His Spirit is active in you when he brings these things to your mind. Allow him to do the work of releasing you from impure love and teaching you to love from a pure heart. Your friendship doesn't have to end; it just has to change to be less important than your friendship with God. His Spirit will show you the way.

Frenemies

A frenemy is a friend with enemy-like tendencies. These wolves in sheep's clothing can be sneaky. One day they are great and normal, and the next they are mean and ugly. They are unpredictable except for the fact that you know you can't count on them to be loving and kind. This happens more with girls than guys, but either way, the danger with a frenemy isn't their actions but your reactions. You can remain pure while your friend is acting as your enemy, but once you reject the voice of God and act on your flesh instead, your relationship becomes impure.

The trouble, then, with a frenemy is what you do or think in response to them. If their actions lead you to bitterness, doubt, depression, anger, worry, fear, or any other rejection of God's love in your life, then they are polluting your life with their sin. So in order to remain pure in the face of a mean friend, you have to respond with the fruit of the Spirit, not with the fruit of your flesh. If you have frenemy trouble, check out Hayley's book *Frenemies: What to Do When Friends Turn Mean*. But for now know that pure friendships aren't perfect, but they do involve you being set on responding to the Holy Spirit's call on your life rather than to the attack on your heart.

Control

Friendship goes wrong when a friend becomes a god— that is, when your friend has more influence in your life than your God does. If you are controlled by your friend, then you are no longer a slave to God, no longer 100 percent his. Friends who demand you do what they want are not pure in their intentions or actions but are poisoning your life with their pride and arrogance. No one should control you except those whom God has placed in your life to care for you. Your parents can control you, your boss can control you, and the police can control you (all within reason and legal limits), but that is because God's Word speaks to their authority over you. But friends have no such authority, and to give it to them is impurity at its worst. You cannot hand over your life to another human being out of selfish intent, and that's just what it is. When you let someone else control you, it's because of what you get out of it. Either a sense of acceptance, popularity, love, or fear drives you to turn your life over to another. When you doubt God's Word and you turn to another human being to give you what you believe you need in life, then you pollute your love for God with love of self. Loving yourself so much that you would actually give up your freedom in order to be thought well of by another person is pride and a rejection of God himself. You cannot please people over God. So if you are being controlled, may these words of Paul in Galatians 1:10 be your life verse: "Am I now seeking the approval of man, or of God? Or am I trying to please man? If I were still trying to please man, I would not be a servant of Christ." **You cannot serve Christ and be controlled by your friend. That's serving two gods, and it can't be done** (see Matt. 6:24).

Talking Too Much

Talking a lot is a sign of impurity, because when you talk a lot you spend most of your time talking about yourself or others. When you talk a lot about yourself you are self-obsessed, and when you talk a lot about others you are most often being critical. Plus, when you talk too much you cannot listen, and listening is often related to selflessness. But failing to listen is making your thoughts more important than others', including God's. Face it, **you can't hear the words that God is speaking while you are talking**. And that's ultimately what makes the one who talks too much impure. Your purity is based on your God, and if you can't hear God because there is never a quiet moment, then where is your purity?

In any relationship there must be times of listening and of talking, but if the talking outweighs listening, then the relationship is in trouble. If you want purity in relationship to your friends, you have to listen as much as you talk and listen with the ears of Christ. What would he hear? Any imbalance and the impure motivation of selfishness invades the relationship.

~~~

It's easy to fall into impure friendships. But if you will remain mindful of the life of Christ in you, and if you will listen to the voice of the Holy Spirit guiding you, producing in you the fruit of the Spirit, then your friendships will approach true purity, and you will remain undivided in your love for the Father.

Enemies

Friendship is more complicated than just hanging out with whoever you like the most. It all actually hinges on the reason for your existence. If you lived to please yourself, then friendship would be organic. It would just happen, and how it happened or who it happened with would be irrelevant. But since you became a believer, you no longer exist to please yourself but live to please your God. That is why the subject of purity is so important. **We are impure in our relationships because we look at them through the lens of our feelings.** But the life of faith is a different filter. The faithful look at relationships through the filter of Christ—his heart, his life, and his love. That's why friendship with the world is not acceptable for the believer, but neither is animosity toward it. God so loved the world that he gave his only son (see John 3:16). And he wants his children to love the world as well, not to hate it. That is why pure faith has no enemies, or at least treats no one as an enemy.

If there are people in your life who hate you, hurt you, or betray you, then you might call them your enemy. You might wish they were dead or at the very least suffering the way they've made you suffer. You might cringe when they come around, you might want others to see how awful they are, or you might just want them to leave you alone. But Jesus says, "Love your enemies and pray for those who persecute you" (Matt. 5:44). *Screech!* Stop the train! What did he just say? Love your enemies? How is that possible? They are the worst people on earth! Dirt—worse than dirt! But no matter how filthy they are, God wants

Hayley's Impure Social Life

When I was in high school my social life was broken. I went to a small school, with just forty in my graduating class, and so we all knew each other very well. Because of my broken ideas on friendship, I soon became the victim of choice for mean girls. See, I had this idea that my social life was more about me than them. That is to say that I didn't consider how others felt but only thought about how I felt as I hid in shyness and fear. I was unsure of myself, so I didn't reach out to others, I didn't get involved in sports, I didn't talk to girls to form bonds with them. I isolated myself and stuck to the boys in the school. After all, they were easier to get along with. They weren't catty or complicated but were cool and simple, and I liked that. Unfortunately, the girls didn't like that, so they did all they could to make my life miserable. If only I had known that life was not about me but about God, things would have been completely different.

you to love him with all your heart, soul, mind, and strength by loving your enemy. After all, if you just loved the people who were nice to you, you'd be no different than the nonbeliever who loves the lovable (see Matt. 5:46–47). But you are God's glory and his image bearer here on earth, meant to show his love to the world, to entice nonbelievers and to impress them with his goodness. So you don't have the luxury of hating your enemies but need to love them.

But how can you love those who you feel so much disgust for? How do you love the ugly, unlovable, and mean people in your life? Well, it starts with the Holy Spirit. His presence in you is the only way that you can love those who hate you. **His Spirit gives you the fruit of the Spirit that is meant to feed the people around you, to nourish them and to point them to Christ.** When you listen to the Spirit's little voice instead of your flesh's loud one, you start to experience stuff like love, joy, peace, patience, kindness, and goodness, and these evidences of the Spirit help you love your enemies. You love them in his strength and not your own. You love them through the power of the Holy Spirit, plain and simple. When an enemy attacks or even just threatens to attack and you have your mind set on the stuff of the Spirit, he reminds you of God's thoughts on love and vengeance. He brings to mind the words of God, "Vengeance is mine" (Deut. 32:35). And when you remember those words, you know that to take vengeance by failing to love your enemy would be to steal something that belongs to God, and so you stop short of such a stupid step.

When you are intent on listening to the Holy Spirit, you hold back from thinking bitter or resentful thoughts about your enemy because you are reminded of the words in Ephesians 4:31, "Let all bitterness and wrath and anger and clamor and slander be put away from you, along with all malice." So when the believer finds themselves with an enemy, they react to that enemy without regard for the acts of the enemy. In other words, they react based on the Holy Spirit and not what the person has done.

When your life is purely, 100 percent dedicated to God and not self, then nothing anyone can do can derail or destroy you. Knowing that God is sovereign, that he has the power over everything in your life, including your enemies, you suddenly find it impossible to take offense at their cruelty. That's because you look to God for every trial in your life, knowing that he works all things together for the good of those who love him (see Rom. 8:28), including even the acts of our enemies. After all, Jesus died for his enemies, for those of us who would reject him and hate him. Still he begged God to forgive us because we didn't know what we were doing. Christ's very life is evidence of God's love for enemies, and it must be our reason for loving as well. Let's take a look at a few of the ways you might not be loving your enemies the way God intends.

Unforgiveness

This might go without saying, but let's just drive this home: Unforgiveness is a terrible thing. We all need forgiveness for our sins; it grants us access to heaven. And the forgiveness you give to those who hurt or hate you is demonstrating God's forgiveness to you. Matthew 6:14–15 makes this clear:

For if you forgive others their trespasses, your heavenly Father will also forgive you, but if you do not forgive others their trespasses, neither will your Father forgive your trespasses.

No matter what other human beings do to you, you must be willing to forgive, especially when they repent and ask your forgiveness (see Luke 17:3–4). But if your enemy shows no remorse, you must still be willing to get over it by letting go and refusing to hold a grudge, to want revenge, or to harbor resentment for them. You must refuse to sin because of them.

If you are living with unforgiveness, then your heart is holding on to impurity, because it isn't fully devoted to God but is divided between his desires and your own. In order to become purely his, reject the feelings you are holding on to and let go. Trust God with your enemy. Pray for them, love them, and let the Holy Spirit work in you to produce the fruit of the Spirit that soothes the angry heart.

Anger

Being angry is a natural human emotion. While anger isn't a sin, acting on it is (see Eph. 4:26). If you are angry because of your enemies that's okay, but you can't let anger be the impulse behind your actions. In other words, you can't say what your anger wants you to say or do what your anger wants you to do. When you do, you follow your flesh, and you shut down the voice of the Spirit and reject God's will in your life. This clouds the water of your purity and makes it toxic. **Anger does more to destroy you than it does to destroy your enemy.** So you can't let anger take hold of your heart. You have to reject it as a selfish emotion that attempts to reject God as Lord of your life and replace him with self. You've got to be "slow to anger; for the anger of man does not produce the righteousness of God" (James 1:19–20). When your heart starts to boil, stop for a second and remind yourself that life isn't about you or what anyone has done to you but is about Jesus and what he has done for you. He has given his life so that you can give yours. "And he said to all, 'If anyone would come after me, let him deny himself and take up his cross daily and follow me'" (Luke 9:23). The Holy Spirit prompts you to reject the call of anger and instead to deny yourself and to follow Christ into love, even love for those who hate you.

Fighting

Arguments happen. Emotions take over and disagreements turn into fights. And while friction is acceptable, fighting is not. Friction is what happens when two surfaces rub up against each other. When a knife rubs against a sharpening stone, the knife gets sharper. So not all friction is bad. Proverbs points to this when it says, "Iron sharpens iron, and one man sharpens another" (Prov. 27:17). Friction is normal, but friction is meant to take off the rough edges and to smooth out the bumps. It's not meant to drive us away from one another in brokenness but to push us toward each other through developing humility and selflessness. **When arguments erupt, the way you can stay pure is by refusing to take the discussion personally** but instead choosing to hear the voice of God in the words of the other. If you can see God working to soften and smooth out your life, then you will no longer be led astray into fighting but will happily look for God's gentle hand of correction and teaching in your life.

"Jesus Christ lived in the midst of his enemies. At the end all his disciples deserted him. On the Cross he was utterly alone, surrounded by evildoers and mockers. For this cause he had come, to bring peace to the enemies of God. So the Christian, too, belongs not in the seclusion of a cloistered life but in the thick of foes. There is his commission, his work. 'The Kingdom is to be in the midst of your enemies. And he who will not suffer this does not want to be of the Kingdom of Christ; he wants to be among friends, to sit among roses and lilies, not with the bad people but the devout people. O you blasphemers and betrayers of Christ! If Christ had done what you are doing who would ever have been spared?' (Luther)."

Dietrich Bonhoeffer, *Life Together: The Classic Exploration of Faith in Community*[1]

When we used to argue—and that used to be a lot of the time—we would end up in a big fight because we both wanted to be right more than anything. But now that we want more than anything to see God at work and for him to shape us, mold us, and smooth us out, our arguments don't erupt into fights because we look for God in each other's words. We want to change, and **change takes place with friction.** Change is uncomfortable but essential in the life of faith. After all, **if God isn't changing you, then he hasn't saved you.** So embrace the chance to change when you disagree with another person, even if that change is simply the change from bitterness to love or from anger to peace. Let change be what you are all about, and your life will be as pure as the driven snow.

How you react to the enemies in your life will either pollute your life or help to purify it. All the relationships in your life can be purified by listening to the still small voice of God. When you respond to the Holy Spirit in you rather than the flesh in you, purity comes easy and your relationships improve. So don't let your enemies define you, but let purity be the best description of you.

Strangers

A pure heart is a heart with the sole goal of loving God with everything and loving one's neighbor as

Therefore

welcome one another

as

Christ has

welcomed you,

for the

glory of God.

Romans 15:7

oneself. But what about when that neighbor is a stranger? How you treat the people you don't know can say more about the purity of your heart than any other relationship. That's because most often strangers are people you don't need anything from. You might be tempted to ignore them or mistreat them because you get nothing out of being kind or gracious to them and you feel you have to get something in order to give something. In other words, how you treat strangers reveals the motive of your love. If you love, show kindness to, or honor only those who love you back or who you hope will one day love you back, then you are expressing impure love, the kind spent on self rather than on God.

Pure love isn't about what you get out of the equation but is about serving God and pointing others to him. Because of this pure desire to love God with everything, caring for people you don't know becomes as important as caring for people you do know. **How you feel about strangers reveals how you feel about Jesus.** As he said in Matthew 25:43, "I was a stranger and you did not welcome me, naked and you did not clothe me, sick and in prison and you did not visit me." How terrible not to understand that God wants us to love the unlovable, to love the strange and unimportant people in our paths. When you fail to care for those who can do nothing for you, you fail to care for Christ. "But when you give a feast, invite the poor, the crippled, the lame, the blind, and you will be blessed, because they cannot repay you. For you will be repaid at the resurrection of the just" (Luke 14:13–14).

In order to stay pure, you have to look beyond yourself and look at the world around you. As you are served by strangers such as checkout clerks, sales associates, and servers, look them in the eye. Care for them. Show them kindness and grace, and consider them more important than yourself. Don't order them around or demand too much of them, but be thankful and gracious and reveal Christ to them by blessing them with kindness. As the hands and feet of Christ, you must learn to be tender with strangers, thoughtful and generous. If you are not, then you are just reinforcing their negative view of Jesus.

When you look at the friendships in your life, ask yourself what they are doing for your purity. Are they helping you to remove the impurities from your life, or are they adding in more junk to pollute your soul? This isn't a question that you can sweep under the rug, hoping for the best but afraid to get a really good look at things out in the light. You have to be willing to put your friendships before the light of God to see if they are pure or teeming with bacteria. Then when you see the floaties, be willing to give them up in order to embrace Christ as the purity in your life.

This idea of letting God purify your friendships comes out in the following words found in 1 Peter 1:22, "Having **purified** your souls by your **obedience** to the truth for a sincere brotherly love, love one another earnestly from a pure heart." In all relationships the believer must love from a pure heart. That means being first completely in love with God, with heart, soul, mind, and strength. If your friendships are lacking in purity, then don't fret—God has an answer. Listen to him speak. Hear his voice, respond to his Spirit, and as you do the purity will return and your relationships will be changed.

If in the fellowship of service I seek to attach a friend to myself, so that others are caused to feel unwanted; if my friendships do not draw others deeper in, but are ungenerous (i.e., to myself, for myself), then I know nothing of Calvary love.

Amy Carmichael[2]

true
purity...

in self

How you think about yourself is either pure or tainted. When your self-image is tainted, all kinds of things can go wrong: low self-esteem, self-hate, selfishness, and the list goes on. All that can mess up your life. But when you realign your focus so your heart is set on God instead of self, amazing things happen. All the time you used to spend worrying about yourself, taking care of yourself, and getting yourself out of trouble—all that "self" time drops and your load lightens.

If your preoccupations that center on "self" are getting you down and you are tired of the worry, the fear, the drama, the depression, and the doubt, then let us take you on a journey and see if giving up your self might actually save it.

Me, My Self, and My Selfishness

Then Jesus told his disciples, "If anyone would come after me, let him deny himself and take up his cross and follow me."

Matthew 16:24

Myself. Yourself. Self is the essence of who you are and the part of you that answers to your desires, your wants, and your needs. Self describes you as an individual with dreams, hopes, and drive. And self is the part of you that either separates you from God or sticks you to him. Let's be honest: self is what you usually think about the most. It's what we *all* think about the most. We wake up thinking about ourselves and go to sleep doing the same. We have needs, after all, and we have to take care of ourselves. We are all adults here, not babies who can let other people take care of us and think about us all day. So it can be really easy to fill yourself up with the things of this world just to stay alive and to get things done.

But you were given your self not to use as you please but to give back to God as an empty space for him to fill up with his Spirit. **God gave you the gift of self for that one purpose: to turn it over entirely, 100 percent, to him.** Unfortunately, self has a loud voice and talks almost all the time, and so self can become a cruel master. Natural, but cruel. When all you think about is yourself, when your self screams at you and wants to be taken care of, it is a very demanding boss. Self is the part of you that stands up and puts its fists on its hips in defiance of God and fights for the things of this world that it thinks are essential to life on this planet. But the truly pure life is a life that is 100 percent free from self. It has died to self and is free to devote itself entirely to one thing: the glory of God the Father.

But what in the world does it mean to die to self? What does that look like? The best way to answer that is to take a look at the opposite of the "dying to self" life, and you can do that by looking for all those words with "self" in them that describe your life. In other words, look for the life of **self-confidence, self-esteem, self-will, selfishness, self-obsession, self-effort, self-promotion, or self-indulgence**. You can tell from the words themselves what the subject of each one is—self! While some of these might sound good and healthy and others not so good and healthy, they all taint the lives of the pure because they involve self more than they involve God.

Let's take self-confidence. Who doesn't want that? It's attractive and comfortable. Life is easy when you are self-confident. You can go anywhere and do anything. Self-confident people are great. But **your self-confidence puts faith in your own ability rather than in God's.** And the same is true about self-esteem. People talk all kinds of talk about self-esteem, how important it is and how tragic it is when it's too low or too high. **That's the trouble with self-esteem: it all centers on self, and because of that it rises and falls with your success and failure.** When it falls because life looks bleak, low self-esteem is shaky ground and leads to stumbling. But when it rises, high self-esteem also leads to falling into arrogance and pride. And both lead to all kinds of impurity in thoughts and deeds.

Michael's Impure Life: Online Edition

I'm a social media junkie. I control myself most of the time now, but in the past I would be on some kind of social media 85 percent of the day. I was reading a hundred blogs a day and commenting on over half of them. I was posting to Twitter and/or Facebook all day long, getting followers and playing the game of social media. But then I started to feel sickened by it. I started to see how it was just about me and myself—getting eyes on me, being heard, making comments, and being smart. Once I decided to turn my life over to God 100 percent of the time, my social media use dropped drastically. And now I strive to make all of the time I spend online time spent serving God. Because of that the stress in my life from trying to be heard and to be known has dropped 100 percent.

Self-will is probably the most obvious area of impurity because self-will is just putting your own will over God's. Willing (or wanting) something so much that you have to have it rejects God's design for your life and so also rejects the idea of giving *all* of your heart to him. In fact, in most cases where self-will is involved, most of the heart is set on self and hardly any is left for God. Selfishness is a twin with self-will. Selfishness doesn't do much thinking but does a lot of acting. It acts like a spoiled brat and makes self the center of the universe. It sees everything in the world as revolving around self and demands that things go its way or else. **Selfishness is the opposite of love** because love wants what is best for others, while selfishness wants what is best for self. **You cannot love God while you are loving yourself.** Some would disagree and say that you have to love yourself in order to love anyone, but that's a lie borrowed from the New Age philosophers and movie stars, not the Word of God. "We love because he first loved us" (1 John 4:19), not because we loved ourselves first. When you love God, that covers all the other love needed. When you love God you care for yourself, including your body and your mind, not out of self-love but out of love for the Father, a love that lives to serve him with everything that is in you. His love is your love when you want only what he wants with no selfish intent.

Masturbation: Self-Indulgence or Act of Safety?

We get a lot of questions about masturbation. It's a touchy topic. Since the Bible doesn't use the word or talk about the act, it's difficult for a lot of people to come to an agreement on its presence in a believer's life. Is it the ultimate self-indulgent act or an activity that keeps you from "needing" to relieve your physical urges with someone else? For most people we talk to, masturbation has become a problem for them because of the compulsion to do it frequently and the places their mind wanders to in fantasy while they're doing it. But the best way to consider this is by asking yourself, as in all things, Is this self-indulgent? Am I doing this to make myself happy? To gratify my flesh? Does this glorify God? The answers to these questions will help you shine the light on the motives behind your physical "needs." Prayerfully ask God for his wisdom in your life and his comfort and grace when you feel you've gone too far.

Self-obsession is another *self* word that quickly muddies the waters of purity. To obsess over something is to think about it all the time, to work to protect it, to comfort it, and to please it. When you are self-obsessed you are all about getting what you want or need. Because of that you forget God's Word when your self demands something that is inconsistent with it. You turn a deaf ear to the voice of the Spirit because the voice of self is so much louder. **The self-obsessed spend most of their waking thoughts on themselves,** and because of that they end up giving most of their heart, soul, mind, and strength to themselves.

Self-effort refers to the strength you put behind getting things done, especially spiritually. Self-effort of the spiritual kind is the idea of works—of doing all you can to be good, to be moral, to follow the rules, and to live up to your values. On the surface this self-will can look great, especially to people who want your outward purity to be preserved. But self-effort attempts to do what only God can do, which is be perfect. **That's why so many abstinence pledges fail to keep people pure—because they most often rely on self-effort.** And the self-effort of determination and devotion to a self-defined boundary, which often changes as feelings change, again leads to failure at the hands of self. That's why we must let Christ be our purity. Abiding in him, being mindful of who he is and what he's done for us, and worshiping him instead of the idols of our effort is how our purity is maintained.

Self-promotion is another disease of self that has taken a lot of us by surprise. It can be easy in a world full of social media to feel compelled to market yourself, to put on a good face for the world, and to impress people with your latest update, check-in, or interest. But the pure heart is too consumed with the life of Christ to be distracted by self-promotion. **Self-promotion is all about self and not at all about God.** When you spend the bulk of your waking hours showing off, bragging about where you are or what you are doing, complaining about someone or something, or even just documenting the minutiae of your daily routine or in any way telling the world the sordid details of your life, then you are in the thick of the self-promoting life and are no longer listening to the promptings of the Spirit who has much greater things in store for you. He wants your mind, he wants your heart, and he wants your attention, and he wants to use those things to serve those around you for his glory, not your own. That means that the pure of heart will consider his promptings and use their time and their media skills to tell the world about him—what he's doing, where he's checking in, what he thinks about this or that. The pure in heart leave self-promotion by the wayside and pick up the ministry of telling the world about the love of God and the wonders of his hands.

Ultimately, all our trouble comes down to self-indulgence. Self-indulgence happens when you say "I deserve it" or "I need this." It comes when you look for things that bring you pleasure, when you feel like you can't control yourself but you have to have what you want. When you arrange your life for comfort, for ease, for acceptance, for entertainment, or for enjoyment, you make life about serving self, not serving God. As the hardcore Jesus freak Andrew Murray put it in his book *The Master's Indwelling*, **"Every time you please yourself, you deny Jesus. It is one of the two. You must please Him only, and deny self, or you must please yourself and deny Him."**[3] Wow, what a thought! How does that make you feel? Angry? Unsure? Excited? Maybe all three? Can you agree or do you disagree? See, purity isn't just about saying no to you-know-what; it's about saying yes to God all of the time—yes, yes, yes!—and saying no to your self-life (see 1 Tim. 5:6 and James 5:5).

Humility

The bottom line is that pure actions come when you have died to everything in you that disagrees with Christ. The pure life is lived purely for him and not

Hayley's Impure Self-Obsession

Most of my life I've been self-obsessed. Before I was a Christian all I had was self, so I guess that makes sense. It's easy to obsess over your only hope for success, hope, and peace. But my self-obsession took out a lot of people along the way. I was so self-obsessed that I once moved out of my apartment without telling my boyfriend at the time where I moved to. We weren't even in a fight or anything; I was just tired of him and was moving on. Ugh! Gulp! I can't believe how cruel I was because I was all about me and my feelings.

for self, and therefore it is lived completely differently than the rest of the world lives. However, it's important to note again that the pure life, living through Christ, is not a perfect life. We all still sin. It's normal for humans to live for self, but those moments when we live for God are supernatural. And because living for God is supernatural, it can't be done by humans alone but must be done by God. That's good news! It means that you don't have to be anybody special to be pure. You just have to agree to allow God to replace self as your master, as your voice of reason and faithfulness. When you allow the Spirit to guide you, to warn you, to comfort you, and to protect you, then self is no longer necessary. Then self can be rejected in favor of something much greater.

This rejection of self is called humility, and it is always present in the life of someone imitating Christ. Without humility you can never truly be pure, because humility is how you give up your right to self in favor of the One who saves. Humility says, "I can't do any of this on my own. I need God. I must have more of him and less of me." **Humility puts self to death and raises Christ to the center of your life.** When this happens your happiness takes a backseat to God. Then when questions come up about things that you might do with your body, with your life, or with your emotions, you make decisions based not on what makes you happy but on what makes God happy.

See how that leads to purity? If your choices aren't about making you feel good but are about loving God and bringing him glory, then making choices becomes easy. You are no longer unsure about boundaries or rules but are consumed with love for your Father.

Wants vs. Needs

In the quest for a pure life it is important to understand the difference between wants and needs. There are really just seven requirements, or needs, in this life, and they are oxygen, water, food, excretion, shelter, sleep, and God. Anything beyond those are things that you might *want* but don't *need* in order to live physically. Yes, God uses human contact with others to give us community, fellowship, and love, but we can survive on a desert island without them. When you start to understand this idea you can start to grasp that **a pure heart never requires more than it needs to live.** The pure heart counts everything beyond these things as blessings—even love and companionship from others, even though they can help us emotionally and spiritually thrive. In other words, when you are pure, Christ is enough and you don't use the word *need* for anything that isn't on that list. As 1 Timothy 6:7–8 says, "We brought nothing into the world, and we cannot take anything out of the world. But if we have food and clothing, with these we will be content."

The impure life creeps in on the back of your wants that disguise themselves as needs. When a want becomes a need, you tell yourself that you have to have it or to do it because if you don't, you'll suffer. When this is your state of mind, it is easy to compromise and to pollute your life.

Self is the master of turning wants into needs. Its nature is to turn tons of stuff into essentials and then to demand them in your life. When this happens you find yourself discontented, depressed, and angry when those so-called needs aren't met. But when your needs are properly defined, you can resist spiraling downward when the things this world says you need don't come to pass. When you aren't popular, when your parents don't let you do what you want to do, when you are rejected, lied about, or even hated, your world doesn't come crashing down because you don't need to be accepted, respected, or loved—you only need God and the essentials for life. All the rest is gravy, should you get it, and it's okay, should you not.

The Need for Respect

Respect from others can be a big deal. You might insist on it in order to love a person, but respect

*When Christ
calls a man, he bids him
come and die.*

Dietrich Bonhoeffer,
The Cost of Discipleship[4]

is not a human need, let alone a human right. In fact, look at the life of Christ. How many did not respect him? But demanding others' respect was never the call of his ministry. When they failed to respect or honor him, he didn't chase after them demanding they change and show him the respect he deserved. He just let them walk away. He let them hate him, abuse him, even kill him. In fact, 1 Peter 2:23 tells us that "When he was reviled, he did not revile in return; when he suffered, he did not threaten, but continued entrusting himself to him who judges justly." Jesus didn't demand to be followed, respected, or honored, and neither do those who call themselves "Little Christs" (Christians).

That means that the pure don't need to be seen or followed, friended or retweeted. They don't need respect. None of these are requirements for life or for happiness. When you turn your wants into needs and make them essential to your contentment and happiness, you walk straight into the arms of impurity because you dilute the strength of your love for God with the stuff of this world. You have to understand that even when respect is commanded by God, it isn't something that you can demand of others, because to demand anything of another human being is to turn your wants into needs and your self into an idol.

Physical Needs

There are a few physical needs in your life—things you have to have, like oxygen and a place to go to the bathroom—but beyond those basic physical needs you can function quite well even if your wants are never met. In fact, **calling your wants needs and deciding that you can't live without them is the essence of impurity** and the source of all the trouble that you have controlling yourself in the area of your body.

God's Word isn't silent on the topic of your body. In fact, in the area of sex, it's quite explicit. But for our discussion the most obvious verse on physical purity is this one: "Among you there must not be even a hint of sexual immorality, or of any kind of impurity, or of greed, because these are improper for God's holy people" (Eph. 5:3 NIV). *Hint* is an interesting choice for the translators to use here because a hint can be as small as or smaller than 0.0001 percent—a tiny speck. That means that in your life there can't be even a speck of the stuff of sexual immorality. So any discussion on sexual impurity is best started where the speck finds its form, and that is in your mind.

Sexual sin starts way before your clothes come off. It starts when you begin to believe, if only in the dark recesses of your mind, that your body and/or emotions have needs that involve the satisfaction of your physical wants and desires. That is to say that **sexual sin starts in your thoughts about the purpose of your body.** If you think your body has been given to you for your enjoyment, then you've taken the first step into hintsville. This hint, or teeny-tiny speck, works its way into your soul like a drop of yeast leavens the whole lump of dough, as we see in Galatians 5:9. This imagery of a hint of yeast working its way through the entire lump of dough is a good one for our talk on impurity. Pure faith involves pure bodies, and **pure bodies belong to people who practice dying to self in order to fully serve God.** In the area of self, impurity is found in the selfishness of wanting to do what has a big physical or emotional payoff. It's easy to see that the source of all premarital sex is selfishness, because the goal becomes the pleasure of a person, not pleasing God and honoring his plan. God made sex to be fun, no question. The trouble comes when that pleasure is sought in an impure relationship, and by that we mean one that is outside of marriage. "But we are in love," you say. "We are planning on getting married one day. Who says there's something wrong with that?" A lot of people, but they don't necessarily give a good reason why. So let's see if we can.

It has to do with purity. God ordained marriage in order to keep couples pure—that is, purely devoted to one another. He prescribes marriage as the answer to infidelity and to children going without parents. That's why he commands purity in marriage (see Heb. 13:4). But when a couple isn't married, there is no purity in the sexual relationship because there is no permanent commitment, no covenant between God and the couple. No pure devotion.

When self is dead set on getting its kicks either from the physical relationship or from the good emotions that follow it, impurity enters the relationship. But the pure heart, being fully devoted to God, finds no self-will tugging at it to leave the path of faith and heeds no cry to take the wide road rather than the narrow one (see Matt. 7:13–14). **Premarital sex has to do with an impure heart split between devotion to self and devotion to God.**

But sexual impurity can also involve self-promotion and self-esteem. When having another person love you, or at least be hot for you, builds your self-esteem or your social status, then self has usurped God as ruler of your life. A lot of relationships get out of control when connecting with another person meets a want that has been defined as a need—a need to make the self feel content, popular, or loved.

But a relationship that stays pure is a relationship set on bringing glory to God. It's focused on loving him so much that neither hormones nor the chance for true love can get in the way of his voice, his call, or his direction. To remain pure in your relationship, you have to start before the relationship begins to build your understanding of who God is and what he has done for you. When you see the depths of his love for you, your love for him consumes you, and when that happens his voice is the only voice you want to listen to.

Not that you won't be tempted. And not that you won't feel a burning desire to connect on a "deeper level" with another human being. But in your temptation you, like Christ, will call on God's Word, see things through truth and not deception, and listen to the promptings of the Spirit within you. Most of the time, you will succeed. You will stay pure. But if you should fail, or if you have already failed, do not lose hope. Some of the most amazing words in Scripture are these: "There is therefore now no condemnation for those who are in Christ Jesus" (Rom. 8:1). Thank God for his grace, but remember that purity is a heart condition; it has to do with the love of your heart. That means that the pure don't take advantage of God's grace by tasting impurity while resting on God's forgiveness. You just can't look forward to grace as permission to sin (see Rom. 6:1).

In 1 Corinthians 6:13, Paul says these important words about your body: "The body is not meant for sexual immorality, but for the Lord, and the Lord for the body." **Your body is not your own.** You gave up your right to it when you opened it up to become a temple of the Holy Spirit. "Or do you not know that your body is a temple of the Holy Spirit within you, whom you have from God? You are not your own, for you were bought with a price. So glorify God in your body" (1 Cor. 6:19–20). Any attempt to go around God's will, to avoid the voice of his pure Spirit, and to indulge in selfish pleasure is toxic to your soul. Pleasure is selfish when it cannot be used to bring glory to God. If what you are doing isn't something that can draw others closer to Christ, and if it isn't a representation of who he is, then it is selfish and it is sinful.

But what about things you do to your body that aren't sexual in nature? Stuff like tattoos, piercings, cutting, binging, purging? Are any of these things impure? We bet you could figure that out without us, but that's not why you bought the book, so here's some help. First of all ask yourself this: "Why do I want to do this? For my glory or his? For my happiness or his?" Your answer will help determine the purity of your heart on this issue. In everything you do with your body, ask yourself, "Does it serve Christ or myself?" The answer to this question is crucial. If you say it serves Christ, then be sure to ask yourself, "In what way?" and then find biblical support or wise Christian counsel for your answer. If you cannot find spiritual support, then chances are that you are serving your own desires over God's.

The Pure Outside

Besides what you do to your body, purity also relates to how you dress your body. **Purity is about not just the flesh but the stuff that hangs on the flesh too.** And like all other aspects of purity, how you dress reveals the devotion of your heart. When you dress to impress for your glory and not God's, you dress for issues related to selfishness and self-esteem. Selfishness in dress comes from dressing for yourself, your taste, your comfort, and your likes, without any regard for others. **The person who dresses with a pure intent dresses to please God over self.** That means that when they dress, they consider the souls of those around them. Is what you are wearing going to cause anyone to stumble when they see you? After all, God's Word has a stern warning on this subject, found in Mark 9:42: "Whoever causes one of these little ones who believe in me to sin, it would be better for him if a great millstone were hung around his neck and he were thrown into the sea" (Mark 9:42). A lot of girls miss it on this idea because they are clueless about how guys think. So bear with us, guys, while we give the girls a little insight into how you tick.

Girls, guys are visual creatures. They are turned on by what they see, and when they see something they like, it can be very easy for them to think about it in ways that lead not only to temptation but to all kinds of sin.

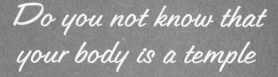

Do you not know that your body is a temple

of the

Holy Spirit within you,

whom you have from God?

You are not your own,

for you were bought with a price.

So glorify God

in your body.

1 Corinthians 6:19–20

Jesus gives us reason to believe this when he says, "But I say to you that everyone who looks at a woman with lustful intent has already committed adultery with her in his heart" (Matt. 5:28). So when a guy even looks at a girl with lust, he's guilty of sin—and in this case, so is the girl who led him to stumble.

But, the opposite can be true as well—girls have eyes and they know how to use them. So guys, how you dress, how you show off your body, and how hard you've been working on your abs can do the same type of damage to the girls around you.

When you are pure, this bothers you. If you find the idea of causing others to sin sickening, then you have just heard from the Holy Spirit, and that's a good thing. Now it's time to respond to his voice and change the way you think about getting dressed in the morning. As in all things, think about your clothes with pure intentions of loving God and loving his children, and then make your decisions. You just might find that a lot of things are impure and need to be dumped. Whether it's because you're showing a lot of skin or because you're using a lot of self-obsessed accessories to draw attention to your individuality, dressing to single yourself out as unique, rebellious, or somehow special is an impure choice. Some people work so hard to look different, to make a statement, that all eyes are on them when they walk into a room. In this case they are drawing attention meant for God onto themselves and so living impure lives.

Pure Personality

But there is more to the pure outside than clothing; there is also personality. **When your heart is set on God over self, your personality begins to change.** The way you used to be is seasoned, freed, or softened as it is tempered by the Holy Spirit. When Hayley was younger she had a flamboyant personality. All attention was on her when she went into a room, and she loved it. She dressed to get attention, always looking different and unique, hoping to stand out. Her laugh was loud, her words were witty and crude, cutting and sassy, but they served her well, or at least she thought so, because of the attention they got her. Later, after she began to sense the call to purity in her life as a call to love God and make him the center of attention, her personality began to change, and the attention she used to covet no longer excited her. Now she no longer tries to get people to be shocked or surprised by her but works at revealing Christ to those around her.

When someone has a loud or brash personality, when they love to talk about anything but God and rarely are at a loss for words, when they like to be the center of attention or to be the life of the party, they are often looking past God to self-obsession, to selfishness, and to self-esteem to please them and to fulfill them. This attempt to draw attention to self is at the root impure because of the emphasis it places on self-glorification over glorifying God. It's not that being the life of the party is a bad thing; it's all a matter of motive. Do you want the attention for your own glory or to serve those around you?

If you feel left out on the personality front because you are a more shy type, never fear, your personality can be purified as well. Those with a quiet and reserved personality can consider their motivation in holding themselves back from others. If your personality is shaped by your fear of rejection, of looking bad, or of embarrassment, then your devotion to God is divided by your devotion to yourself and your concern about what people think about you. The heart that loves God with its all doesn't put self-protection above God's desire for you to serve and love others, to speak to them of his love, and to open yourself up to develop relationships with those around you that might lead to their finding their way to the foot of the cross.

The purpose of your life, of your body, and of your self isn't to please your self but to serve, work for, and love God with all of your strength. So in all areas of your life your love for God must compel you to decrease so that he might increase (see John 3:30). If you sense the Holy Spirit's call on your life right now, then jump at the chance to start anew to deny your self-life and embrace Christ's life in you.

Are you living in your purpose? Have you completely turned yourself over to God to be filled with his Spirit? If not, then let today be the day when you commit yourself 100 percent to loving him. Impurity isn't just a question of doing you-know-what but has just as much to do with the things you have believed were needs, or at least very important wants. When your selfish interests start to dominate your life, informing your decisions and coloring your actions, then your love for God is impure. Out of that impurity comes the kind of stuff that puts you in bondage to your very own flesh, and with that comes death, as we see in Romans 8:13: "For if you live according to the flesh you will die, but if by the Spirit you put to death the deeds of the body, you will live" (Rom. 8:13). Don't let yourself be fooled. Living to serve self leads to an impure life and ultimately to spiritual death. But you can be free today—free to live and free to love if you are just willing to die to self and to bury yourself in the life of Christ, choosing to give everything you are, everything you were, and everything you will be over to his Spirit so that you might never again live for self.

true
purity...

in mind

*W*hat's on your mind? Are you happy with it? Happy with your thoughts? Your obsessions? The things that occupy your mind? How you think affects your entire life—how you feel, what you do, even how others react to you. Your mind is really the beginning of it all. Your mind is where you make the decision to give your life over to Christ or to keep it for yourself. And it's where you decide what this world means to you and how much it will influence you.

Sometimes your mind can seem beyond your control. It can wander off, lose focus, or take you places you never wanted to go. So surrendering control of your mind to God is important not only for your sanity but also for your soul and even for your body. Did you know that the things you think about can actually make you sick? Think about how an ulcer is the symptom of a mind that worries a lot. Or how fear can change your temperature, blood pressure, and heart rate. Your mind is a powerful thing, and understanding it and using it to its fullest and most godly capacity can greatly improve your life and glorify God.

The Power of the Mind

In the Bible the word *mind* is often interchangeable with *heart*. Most people use the word *heart* to refer to our feelings, but in Scripture the person is seen as a whole, not separate parts, so it frequently uses *heart* to include your mind, your heart, and even your soul. When the Bible says in Proverbs 4:23, "Above all else, guard your heart, for everything you do flows from it" (NIV), it is also telling you to guard your mind because everything else—including feelings, actions, personality—comes out of it.

Your mind with all of its thoughts, then, essentially defines you. Whatever you choose to think about the most determines your actions and your feelings, and many times even your personality. Your mind is the beginning of it all. In your mind you think thoughts about God, and in your mind you make decisions, choices that your body and emotions then act upon. So your mind must be focused on the purity of Christ and what he did on the cross in order for your life to be based on the same purity.

When your mind is set on the things of the Spirit, God speaks through his Word and you listen. And as you listen, you grow the fruit of the Spirit. So the person whose mind is set on God is growing more and more in the areas of love, joy, peace, patience, kindness, goodness, faithfulness, gentleness, and self-control (see Gal. 5:22–23). When your mind is set on the things of God, you are filled with hope rather than discouragement and with rest rather than busyness. Your mind-set determines your life—how you live it and what you do with it. Your mind is essential to your faith, because what you use your mind for and what you think about, daydream about, or fantasize about determines your purity.

Mind Control

According to Scripture your mind isn't free. It's controlled, either by your flesh or by the Spirit. And Romans 8:6 tells us that "letting your sinful nature control your mind leads to death. But letting the Spirit control your mind leads to life and peace" (NLT). When people set their minds on their sinful nature, or flesh, they think they are free—free from rules, free from dogma, free from a God who tells them what to do. But the truth is that they are not free at all; they are slaves. The stuff they choose to do and choose to believe quickly begins to consume them. For example, the guy who wants to be free to experiment with drugs, to do whatever feels good, quickly finds himself a slave to the very thing he once thought was his freedom. And the girl who wants to be free to let her body go and be with anyone she wants to

*For as he
thinks in his heart,
so is he.*

Proverbs 23:7 NKJV

be with quickly finds out that she too is a slave to her obsession for more.

No one is free. Either you're a slave to Christ, bought with his blood, devoting yourself to him, or you find yourself obsessed with and controlled by your flesh. All of this is because you were made to obsess. Obsess is what the pure do. If you are 100 percent *for* something, you are obsessed with it, consumed by it, given over to it with all your heart, soul, mind, and strength. That's the point of this book: you were made to be consumed with, or controlled by, your love for God, and it all starts in your mind.

As we see in Romans 8:9, "You are controlled by the Spirit if you have the Spirit of God living in you" (NLT). When the Spirit lives in you, he informs you, he guides you, he teaches you. And as you listen to and respond to the Spirit, you are controlled by the Spirit, and the flesh loses its power. **The pure are not those who set their minds on their actions but are those who set their minds on God himself** (see Col. 3:2). You cannot be pure by setting your mind on the things of the flesh. In other words, you aren't pure because you keep your flesh from going too far or doing this or not doing that. Even people without the Spirit can control themselves in some areas of their lives, but **you are pure when you respond to the Spirit rather than the rule** (see Rom. 3:20; Gal. 5:18).

The Spirit wants all of your mind on him. He wants to consume you. When this happens you are said to be walking by the Spirit. And Galatians 5:16 says, "Walk by the Spirit, and you will not gratify the desires of the flesh." When you walk by the Spirit, your mind is led by the Spirit. That means that you go wherever the Spirit goes, you listen to his voice, you look for his will, and you follow his counsel. When you do this, Galatians tells you, you won't give in to the flesh with all its wants and desires. You won't live by the flesh because your mind won't be set on it but will be set on God. And when your mind is set on God you find life, freedom, and peace. This freedom we read about earlier in Galatians 5:13, which says, "For you were called to freedom, brothers. Only do not use your freedom as an opportunity for the flesh." **To be controlled by the Spirit is actually to find freedom**, while to let the flesh do whatever it wants in its so-called freedom is actually bondage. Second Peter 2 talks about those things people think they are free to do and says that "whatever overcomes a person, to that he is enslaved" (v. 19).

Your mind will be controlled, either by the flesh or by the Spirit. As believers, we are able to rip free from the bondage to the flesh and all its cravings, fears, and worries by allowing our minds to be led by the Holy Spirit, responding to his voice and answering his call.

So how does it happen? How does your mind stay pure and not get polluted by the flesh or the stuff of this world? It's an important question, and answering it can save you a lot of heartache. See, the things of this world were never meant to control you, to scare you, or to worry you. But fear, worry, doubt, and hopelessness all show up when your mind is impure—when you are no longer consumed with Christ but with life. So let's take a look at how to avoid this kind of impure distraction in your mind and life.

Pure Peace

In this busy world there can be lots of anxiety and stress. So much to do, so little time. And the stuff you have to do can seem unbearable, exhausting, even impossible. Because of that your mind can go into a tailspin and sometimes even take your body along with it. Problems like headaches, ulcers, colds, insomnia, indigestion, and all kinds of other physical junk can be blamed on the impure thoughts we have over the things the world demands of us.

But the pure mind is set free from this stuff. When you take your mind off the stuff of this world and put it onto Christ, you are promised peace. Isaiah 26:3 says to God, "You keep him in perfect peace whose mind is stayed on you, because he trusts in you."

See the correlation? **Perfect peace is available for all who keep their minds on God.** When you trust him, as it says in the second half of the verse, you commit yourself fully to him—not partially but purely. So the pure mind is the peaceful mind.

Is your mind stressed out? Are you getting sick and tired of the anxiety you are living in? Then consider the fact that it's all because your mind is divided, not focused on God. That's good news, because the first step to change is knowing what the problem is. Your heart knows it's true: your mind is consumed with the stuff of the world, and it's wearing you out. Let the Holy Spirit work in you. Let him teach this stuff to your heart. You can't do it by yourself. You can't get away from the pull of this world or make peace come into your life in your own strength. But with the Holy Spirit, you can. Thanks to his strength and not your own, peace can be yours all the time, in any situation.

So if you want peace, then look no further than the Spirit of God. In him you have everything you need. Make these words stick in your mind so they are always present and you can always repeat them: "Do not be anxious about anything, but in everything by prayer and supplication with thanksgiving let your requests be made known to God. . . . And the God of peace will be with you" (Phil. 4:6, 9).

Pure Eyes

Have you ever noticed that you can't seem to concentrate on anything else when your eyes are uncomfortable? Your eyes are the windows of your body. It's through them that all the light enters. They are important to your entire being—so important that Jesus even had something to say about them. In Matthew 6:22 he says, "The eye is the lamp of the body." That means that "if your eye is healthy, your whole body will be full of light" (Matt. 6:22). Healthy here literally means "single," focused, pure. If your eye is pure, your whole body will be full of the light of God.

So how do you keep your eyes pure? How do you let in only the light of God and not the darkness of the world? This is an important question because there are so many opportunities to be impure just by opening your eyes. Once you set your eyes on something, your mind starts to think about it. It imagines it, remembers it (sometimes forever), and forces your mind to make decisions about it. **The more your eyes look at something, the more acceptable it becomes to your mind.** And that means the less it strikes you as impure or worldly. It can be easy to see evil when it's out of the ordinary or shocking, but when you slowly look at more and more impure things, your mind gets used to them, and soon you don't see the evil in them at all.

This happens a lot in the area of sexual images. When you see a sexual image, at first you might be shocked as your mind realizes it's seeing something it shouldn't see. But if you see that kind of image enough times, you will see less and less wrong with it as your mind becomes desensitized to sin. But God wants us to keep the lights on, not hide in the dark and look at sexy pictures. In Romans 13:13 we read, "Let us walk properly as in the daytime, not in orgies and drunkenness, not in **sexual immorality** and **sensuality**, not in quarreling and jealousy." You might not call looking at porn sexual immorality—after all, you aren't doing anything other than looking—but if you apply Jesus's words on lust from Matthew 5:28, you are doing all you need to do in order to be in sexual sin: "But I say to you that everyone who looks at a woman with lustful intent has already committed adultery with her in his heart." But wait, there's more: the verse also mentions sensuality, which is the act of indulging your senses, or in other words doing anything that involves self-gratification—pleasing yourself, giving yourself a good time, as it were, even if only with your eyes or in your mind. It's all the same, and it involves polluting the waters of your soul with self.

So the mind has to be guarded. You can't use it for your pleasure or for your release or escape, because when you escape from God you run from the only one who can save you. But sex isn't the only kind of escape; there are many others. Escape can be anything that your eyes like to stare at that tempts you to sin. If you're a shopaholic and you stare at fashion magazines every month, or if you're obsessed with the latest pop star and you gaze at their photo all day long, you are setting your mind on your temptation and encouraging it to jump right in and sin.

Pure eyes look at life differently. Pure eyes are guarded from the filth of this world. They spend their waking moments looking into the things of God and informing your mind of all things good and excellent. If your eyes are tempted to look somewhere that causes you to sin, then stop today and listen to the voice of the Holy Spirit. You can break any obsession by replacing it with the obsession you were made for. Turn to God and allow his Spirit to convict you, to change you, and to heal you.

Pure Thoughts

The thoughts you think determine the feelings you feel. The two go hand-in-hand. Think good thoughts and have good feelings; think bad thoughts and, well, you can figure it out. But in any discussion about purity, when we talk about loving God with all your heart, soul, mind, and strength, we have to talk about your thoughts. Does this all-consuming love for God mean he's all you think about every minute of the day? If so, then how do you concentrate on your other work at hand? How do you study, practice, and work when all you think about is God? These are some important things to consider. Let's see if we can't help you better understand what it means to have pure thoughts.

Philippians 4:8–9 gives a great description of pure thinking, and it goes like this: "Finally, brothers, whatever is true, whatever is honorable, whatever is just, whatever is pure, whatever is lovely, whatever is commendable, if there is any excellence, if there is anything worthy of praise, think about these things. What you have learned and received and heard and seen in me—practice these things, and the God of peace will be with you." This direction for the mind is one of the most valuable instructions in all of Scripture, because it speaks directly to how your thoughts remain pure. Notice what it says about the kinds of things to think about. The first and most important thing is whatever is true. Most of the stress in your life comes when you think something that is untrue. Like "This thing in my life is going to kill me," "I can't handle the strain," "Rejection is the worst thing in the world," "I deserve more than I am getting," "No one loves me," "I'll never be happy," "The future is a scary place," and so on. These lies, when taken as truth, deceive your heart into believing them and your emotions into acting on them. Then out of these lies come all kinds of bad and often uncontrollable feelings.

But the remedy for these feelings is found in this passage. When you reject the lies and accept the truth that the Holy Spirit is sharing with you, the darkness becomes light and the strain of the lies is lifted. If what you are thinking isn't a biblical truth; if it isn't honorable or just; if it rejects God, his sovereignty, his omnipotence, his goodness, or his love; if it is ugly, bad, or not worthy of praise, then you must allow the Holy Spirit to replace the lies with truth. **You must stop shutting him out with your negative self-talk and shut up and listen, allowing him to pour truth back into your heart through His Word and to purify you through that truth.** This imagery is seen in Ephesians 5:26 where it says of Jesus and the church that he has "cleansed her by the washing of water with the word."

In this life you are going to have to do things that are not necessarily spiritual, and your mind will need to concentrate on things other than God. But your thoughts can stay pure when they don't get derailed by lies because you don't start to complain to yourself about your life or the things you have to do, but instead you follow 1 Corinthians 10:31: "Whatever you do, do all to the glory of God." As you focus your purpose on him, direct all of your effort toward that purpose, and do all that you do in the

Hayley's Impure Mind

Before I learned the truth I believed a lot of lies. They made sense to me and were confirmed by most of the world, so I went with it. But once the lies started to turn darker, convincing me that I was worthless because my dad left me and that I should just kill myself to save the world from having me in it, I started to get scared. What were these thoughts, and why were they so bent on destroying me? The answers came as I started to learn the difference between the voice of the Holy Spirit and the voice of my flesh. My flesh gave me thoughts of tragedy, desolation, and destruction. My flesh spoke of the mess of it all, while the Spirit speaks of the God who rules over it all. Knowing the difference between the voice of your flesh and the voice of God is the only way to get free from the lies of your mind. And the first step is spending time in his Word.

strength of the Holy Spirit, then no matter what your mind must concentrate on, it will remain pure, totally devoted to the Father.

When you are loving God with all your heart, soul, and mind, then your thoughts are all pleasing to him. And when everything you do is done for him, then you are loving him with all of your strength.

Pure Trust

Doubt is not a part of love, and love isn't reserved just for the good people in your life but is meant for the lousy ones as well. This might come as a shock to you. You might think that trusting people is not only dangerous but impure. And while trusting them more than you trust God can be both of those things, trust is a healthy and faithful response to the people God has put in your life. How can we say that? Because God's Word says that to love him with all your heart, soul, mind, and strength includes loving your neighbors. And 1 Corinthians 13:7 describes love using these words, "It always protects, *always trusts*, always hopes, always perseveres" (NIV).

But how do you trust someone who has failed you often? And why should you risk being hurt again, taken advantage of, or made a fool of? The answer to that depends on your definition of love. If you take God's definition, then you have to deal with the verse that says love always trusts. This is one of the things that makes Christian love so different than any other love. And it's one of the things that makes the Christian's mind, the mind of Christ, so pure. Rather than getting all caught up in self-protection and the desires of the flesh, the mind set on Christ trusts him so much that when he says to trust someone, you do. That means that even though others fail you, even if they are sinful and cruel, you don't make that an excuse to stop loving them by doubting that they are lovable. In other words, **doubt excludes people from your love by making them seem unlovable.** But God doesn't put anyone on the unlovable list. In fact, you know that he goes so far as to even command you to love your enemies and to pray for those who hate you (see Matt. 5:44). **Doubt accuses people of future sin** and leaves no room for grace or for change, both of which God majors in.

When Hayley was a kid, her dad left her, and she doubted him for many years. This doubt led her to accuse him of not loving her, of rejecting her, and of neglecting her. These ideas about him made her angry, bitter, and hateful, emotions that wreak havoc on a mind. She doubted his love for her, and so in return she decided not to love him. But when she found the grace to forgive him for being a sinful human, and when she could stop doubting his love because of his actions and start believing in him and trusting him to love her the best way he knew how, then she allowed God to be God and stepped down from the throne. This notion that she had to protect herself through doubt was a lie. God never encourages doubt. But love always trusts and always hopes for a better tomorrow. When you realize this, things begin to change, first in your mind and then in your life.

God doesn't want you to have the kind of trust in people that joins in with the sins of this world but instead the kind of trust that insists on purity as it loves sinners and rejects their sin. You can trust others by not allowing their sin to pull you into sin but instead praying for them, caring for them, and trusting that God can redeem them and save them from themselves. Don't allow your doubts about people to lead you to doubts about God and his Word, but stick to the faith. Trust God and trust his Word—it is truth and it can be trusted.

You cannot have pure trust while your mind is divided between truth and lies. It is essential that you know the truth so that the lies don't entice you to believe them, because lies destroy your life. They make you believe the worst when all is as it should be. They make you think things that are untrue and therefore useless or even destructive. But in order to spot a lie you have to know the truth, the truth Jesus was talking about

Michael's Impure Trust

For me, my doubt about people shows itself in anger and frustration. I am prone to anger when I see people do stupid stuff, and I doubt their sanity. It's really easy for me to be mad at people who do things I would never do. It's not my nature to trust God or them when I see ridiculousness happening. If I had been around Jesus when he walked on the earth, I would have been like Peter—I would have been correcting Jesus and trying to protect him, because some of the stuff he did would have made no sense to me. But as I study true purity, I'm learning to trust that God is sovereign and to accept the "stupid" in people as quite possibly something God allowed in my life to teach me a concept he wants me to learn. Because I'm stupid to the ways of God too.

when he said, "You will know the truth, and the truth will set you free" (John 8:32 NLT). The truth Jesus was talking about is himself. He called himself "the way, and the truth, and the life" in John 14:6. So you have to know Jesus, not just know about him. And the way you know him is through his Word, the Bible. The Scriptures are the truth as well. As you start to consume more and more truth, the lies around you and inside you become obvious. They stand out as rubbish, and you want nothing to do with them. So if you want to get to the bottom of things, if you want to stop believing the lies that make you doubt the hand of God in your life, then get to know the truth. Not someone else's, but God's. Find out who he is and what he has said, and your trust will grow and so will your purity.

The pure mind is blind to anything but the hand of God. It is blind to impossibilities and doubt, as it only sees the One who can. It knows nothing of failure, because it trusts him and believes his Word, which says, "Who has spoken and it came to pass, unless the Lord has commanded it? Is it not from the mouth of the Most High that good and bad come?" (Lam. 3:37–38). Knowing that everything in your life first passes through God's hands should be a major comfort since we know that God is perfect, and so are all his ways. We also know that he loves his children (see John 3:16) and only gives them what is best for them (see Jer. 29:11), so we can know that no matter what happens, he will work all things together for the good of those who love him (see Rom. 8:28).

When your mind is set on yourself and your desires and things go bad, your first impulse can be doubt. You might doubt your chances, you might doubt your purpose, or you might doubt your value in this world. You might even doubt God. But when your mind is set on the Father and things go wrong, your first thought is not doubt but interest in seeing what God is doing. You might wonder, but you do not doubt, because you only want what he wants, and you know that God always gets what he wants. As we see in Daniel 4:35, "Everyone who lives on earth is nothing compared to him. He does whatever he wishes with the army of heaven and with those who live on earth. There is no one who can oppose him or ask him, 'What are you doing?'" (GW). This is the blessing of a pure mind: never needing to accuse him by asking "What are you doing?" because you know he doesn't need your counsel or disapproval in order to manage the world. When your heart is fully set on God, you see only an opportunity for faith and never for complaint or doubt. Your faith in him is your freedom.

Your thoughts are the place where the pure life starts. Without pure thoughts from the mind of Christ, you will not have a pure heart. Pure thoughts are those that trust God and focus on his

Word and his voice. When your mind is set on the things of the Spirit, when you are intent on hearing his voice and responding to it, then your faith is pure and your heart is too.

Pure Courage

Courage isn't the absence of fear but action in the presence of it. When you are courageous it is because you disobey your flesh with all its panic and distress, and you don't freak out. Where there is no fear there is no courage. No one could ever call you courageous for picking up a cute little puppy, because there is nothing to fear from a puppy. So courage isn't about being strong or sure of yourself but is about trusting God more than your fear. It is about agreeing with the words of the psalmist and saying, "The Lord is on my side; I will not fear. What can man do to me?" (Ps. 118:6).

Pure courage comes from pure fear. Not the divided kind that fears the people or the things of this world as much as it fears God. But pure courage rests on these words: "The fear of the Lord is the beginning of wisdom; all those who practice it have a good understanding. His praise endures forever!" (Ps. 111:10). When your mind is focused on one thing, undivided, undistracted by the dangers of this world but bent on fearing only one thing—rejecting God—then courage comes naturally. See, the things of this world that threaten you have no power over you and so can do you no real harm when you don't live for yourself but keep your heart set fully on living for Christ. When you live for Christ, you die to the things of this world that used to control you and paralyze you. The fears that used to direct your steps no longer have influence over you because they impact your flesh, and you no longer have your mind set on your flesh because it is now set on the Spirit. From this mind-set comes life and peace because you know you can no longer be threatened with the fear of this world.

This means that the pure mind doesn't fear any person, because fearing what someone can do to you is setting your mind on the things of this world. When you fear people's disapproval or rejection, or when you fear them taking what's yours or seeing who you really are, you divide your affections between God and people. That's why we can say that fear points to what, or who, you worship. If you fear people, then you have placed too much importance on them and their influence in your life. You have bought the lie that what people think of you or do to you determines your destiny, as if they have some kind of control over who you are or what you do or become. But when you fear God, your fear is based on the truth that only God determines your fate. The truth is that "a person cannot receive even one thing unless it is given him from heaven" (John 3:27). It's not people who decide what happens to you but God. So why fear the powerless rather than the all-powerful?

A pure mind isn't divided in its fear. But when you set your mind on him, when you want only to please and serve him, then fear is un-tainted by the creation and set squarely on the Creator. Don't allow your fear to become distracted by the powerless, but let the fear of not loving God and accepting his grace and kindness be your inspiration for living.

Pure Truth

When you are in a court of law, they ask you to tell the whole truth and nothing but the truth. Anything less than the truth and the system fails. The same is true for your mind: anything less than the truth and your mind will be clouded and confused, easily distracted and led astray. But when you fill your mind with truth, your thoughts are pure.

The single most important truth for your mind is the truth about God. What you believe about God says more about you and your future than anything else in the world. Your thoughts on God will affect your emotions, your actions, your body, and your eternity. As A. W. Tozer said in his phenomenal book *The Knowledge of the Holy*, "Without doubt, the mightiest thought the mind can entertain is the thought of God, and the weightiest word in any language is its word for God."[5] In order to have a pure mind, you must believe the truth about God.

If you aren't sure what you believe about God; if you have mixed emotions; if your thoughts on him are colored by your life experiences; or if you doubt his love, kindness, goodness, forgiveness, or power, then your thoughts on him are impure. These impure thoughts are sure to affect every area of your life. When your thoughts are divided, torn between faith in God and uncertainty of his goodness, your life will always be filled with turmoil. But there is an answer to your trouble, and that is knowledge. In order for your mind to be pure it must be set on God, and in order to be set on him you must know him. You cannot love him if you do not know him. So in order to have pure thoughts about God you must have truthful thoughts about him. You must be convinced that he is who he says he is; that he is all-powerful, all-knowing, and always present; that is he love; and that he is merciful, kind, good, self-existent, self-sufficient, unchanging, and perfect. If you doubt any of these attributes of God, your thoughts are impure. So find out who he is. Listen to his Spirit that will inform you, read his Word and sit at his feet and learn. Purify your mind by setting it on him, and the impurity will fall away from your life.

Pure Imagination

When you were a kid you used your imagination to create kingdoms, to build castles, and to slay dragons. Your imagination was always active, always on. But as you got older those thoughts were replaced with more mature thoughts. You stopped playing pretend, or at least you think you did. The truth is that a lot of us keep living in our imaginations long into adulthood when in our minds we daydream, fantasize, or pretend we have a life beyond our real life. **Fantasizing about another person, a perfect life, or a sudden rise to fame fills your mind with wants and desires for things that aren't yours.** And that is the recipe for discontentment and regret. When your mind is busy in its fantasy it is not focused on God, and when your mind is diverted to your fabricated or fake life, it rejects the gifts of God and instead lives in a place filled with the people and things that God never thought were best for you to have today, or maybe even ever.

You cannot have a pure mind when you are imagining yourself somewhere other than where God has placed you, because that accuses God of unfaithfulness and failure. But the pure imagination sees God's hand in reality, hears his voice in his Word, and senses his touch on the experiences of life. We aren't saying that to imagine something is a sin, but your imagination messes with your mind when you begin to serve it, to obey it, to

Take
every thought
captive to
obey Christ.

2 Corinthians 10:5

hope in it, and to spend your energy on it. If what you imagine is sinful, then as Jesus says, you sin (see Matt. 5:28). The mind isn't off-limits to God. It isn't exempt from judgment. And it cannot be the place you go to enjoy the sins of this world.

Transforming Your Mind

We naturally think like the world does, and we can fix that way of thinking only supernaturally, as we see in 2 Corinthians 3:18, "And we all, with unveiled face, beholding the glory of the Lord, are being transformed into the same image from one degree of glory to another. For this comes from the Lord who is the Spirit." Did you get that? This transformation, this change in your mind, comes from the Spirit. It isn't hard work on your part but is a continual returning of your thoughts to him, reminding yourself who he is and what he has done, and then saying no to anything that lies to you about who he is or what he has done. As 2 Corinthians 10:5 says, "We destroy arguments and every lofty opinion raised against the knowledge of God, and take every thought captive to obey Christ." As you take thoughts captive you break their spell on you, and you turn your mind to truth. In this way the Holy Spirit changes your heart to align with his, and your mind refuses to allow lies to re-direct or control it.

Purity cannot be ordered or forced. No one can insist on your purity in order to keep you pure. Forced behavior isn't pure because the one who is forced didn't make up their own mind to behave that way. So your purity cannot be your parents' purity; it must be your own. Your mind must be set on the things of God. If it is only your actions that are pure as the driven snow but your mind longs for something a little more muddy brown, then all the things you do or don't do are irrelevant. But when your mind truly longs for the only thing that is truly pure, then purity is truly yours—not your parents' or your youth pastor's.

Don't let purity be assigned to you. Realize that Christ in you is your purity and then devote yourself fully to him, rejecting everything else as a diversion from the most important thing your mind could ever do: think rightly about God.

true
purity...

in faith

A lot of the thoughts and talk about purity center more on doubt than on faith. You doubt you know what God wants of you. You aren't sure how far is too far, what you can do, or what you should do, and so you doubt, you fret, and you wonder. But all of this just divides your heart more as you labor over what you have to do to be good. What is expected of you? What have you done wrong? All these things can consume you and even make you question your faith. When your faith wavers—when you have questions, doubts, and fears—it just means you haven't come to the realization that it isn't so much about you but is all about him.

When we were younger we didn't know any of this stuff about purity. Sure, we loved Jesus, we believed in him and knew he was real and died on that cross, but we didn't know the depths of that love or the significance of it for our lives. So we added to it by trying to make rules about purity and how to maintain it. Hayley became so devoted to her "how far is too far" list, guarding it and arguing with boys who wanted to adjust it, that once she broke down and went over the line, going over it again became easier and easier. And guilt became more and more thick in her life, muddying the waters of her faith like a rainy day on the Mississippi River.

Michael thought that being pure in God's eyes meant making everyone happy, pleasing people, a selfless approach to life. But this people-pleasing nature of his led him down some stupid paths, including a quick marriage and divorce and an addiction to gambling. He had worked so hard at saying and doing what others wanted to hear and see that the pressure built up inside until he felt he needed release. He started to hate the life that he had handed over to others, so he ended up becoming the guy he never wanted to become.

Our fatal mistake in the hunt for purity was making purity about a list of things we were doing or not doing rather than about what God had done. We forgot that he had sent his Son to live a perfectly pure life and to become our purity in God's sight. That purity was a free gift; it didn't need to be earned. When your efforts to be pure are based on faith in yourself to "be good," rather than on your faith in God and your deep love for him, you are bound to fail. This can start to take shape when too much of your effort is spent on talking about, defining, and defending your purity. If you feel compelled to do this, then something is consuming you that was never meant to consume you. **No single part of faith is meant to become an obsession—no part but Jesus himself.** So when you stand on something other than Christ as proof that you are pure, you dilute your faith with your own self-will and effort. And you are sure to fail, to fall down, to mess up, and to struggle as long as you put your faith in your own strength of will.

Pure faith is consumed with the person of Christ. This pure faith in him and nothing more cleanses your heart as it is set fully on him (see Acts 15:9). When your heart is no longer divided but is focused with all its energy and strength on your God, you have no need for pledges or rings because your heart is his no matter what you sign or wear. This faith comes from love for the Father and what he has done, and out of that love then comes the obedience that not only you but your parents are looking for. It's a faith that no one can miss when they look at your public and private life.

Faith Loves God

When Hayley was a little girl, she adored her father. He was her idol. He was super cool, super smart, strong, just awesome. She adored him, and because of that love for him she wanted nothing more than to please him. It was easy to be good, to not get into trouble, because she wanted him to be happy because she felt so loved. This is a picture of the life of faith. **We don't obey God to make him love us or save us; we obey him as a natural outpouring**

in response to his love for us. We love him and want nothing more than to please him, and out of that comes joyful obedience. First John 5:3 puts it this way: "For this is the love of God, that we keep his commandments. And his commandments are not burdensome." Your love for him energizes your obedience. And that's what keeps you pure—not your commitment to purity but your love for the One who made you pure.

See, **purity is about loving God over your self because of what he has done for you.** You love him so much that you want no part of self-gratification or the kind of pleasure that isn't in his will. **When your faith grows out of your love for him, living a pure life isn't a strain or a struggle but is a joy that fits as naturally as a glove.** In fact, it is living outside of his will that cuts and chafes as it poisons your love for him. So why do the faithful need the impure life? Why do they need sensual distractions, impure relationships, or self-obsession? They don't, because the impure life serves love for self over love for God. But the faithful find great joy in serving God alone in everything they say or do. This is pure faith.

Faith Doesn't Run Away

Faith doesn't run when things get tough, but faith stays put. It stays put on Christ. In other words, it doesn't

look for a way out that isn't Christ himself. It doesn't look for a break from Christ
but stays focused on him, trusting him and
listening to him. This is what most Bibles
translate as "abiding" when Jesus says,
"Abide in me, and I in you" (John 15:4). To
abide or "dwell" in Christ is to become one with
him as you allow his Holy Spirit to inform your
decisions and your thoughts. This abiding changes
things. It changes the sting of suffering and pain; it
changes the meaning of life. And it changes the way
you make decisions that affect your purity.

First John 2:6 talks about this abiding when it says,
"Whoever says he abides in him ought to walk in the same
way in which he walked." This makes sense, because if
you are ever mindful of him, listening to the promptings
of his Spirit rather than your flesh, then you will naturally
walk the way he walked. And you will be pure as he is pure.
First John 3:9 goes on to give us the amazing news that "No
one born of God makes a practice of sinning, for God's seed
abides in him, and he cannot keep on sinning because he
has been born of God." That might sound impossible to
you—after all, you've read that there is no one righteous,
not even one (see Rom. 3:10), and you've experienced
firsthand the sinfulness of your own heart. So how is it
possible that you no longer make a practice of sinning?
It is possible because as God's seed abides in you,
lives in you, talks to you, and brings his will to your

mind, and you abide in him, listening and setting your heart on loving him, repeating sin as a perpetual habit becomes unfathomable. Sure, you may fall into sin, you might fail to do what you want to do, as Paul described himself doing in Romans 7, but you will not *live* in sin, because you are living in Christ.

Faith stays put; it abides. It doesn't sin and then determine to live there; to ignore God on one count but obey him on all others. That kind of deliberate and willful sin is inconsistent with abiding in Christ. And so the willful sin of living in sexual immorality by moving in with someone, of choosing to have sexual relations with them, or even of choosing to marry a nonbeliever even though God's Word forbids it (see 2 Cor. 6:14) is choosing to live not in Christ but in deliberate sin. And for that there is no sacrifice that can be made, as we see in Hebrews 10:26–27: "For if we go on sinning deliberately after receiving the knowledge of the truth, there no longer remains a sacrifice for sins, but a fearful expectation of judgment, and a fury of fire that will consume the adversaries." How do you know if you are sinning deliberately? If you have heard the truth and yet you feel no remorse for your sin but decide to continue in it, that's deliberate sin. Those who abide in Christ feel remorse and want to change; they don't accept the sin but confess it and work to avoid it in the future by worshiping

God instead of the idol they have created in their heart.

As you abide in Christ, the desire to repent, to stop living in sin, consumes you. As that happens the sin becomes disdainful and you just don't want it anymore. That is when your faith is pure: when you no longer want the things in your life to be inconsistent with the life of Christ in you. It's not when you want your parents to be proud or when you want to fit in with everyone else who's making a pledge for something, but truly pure faith is when you want only what Christ wants and nothing else. When that is your goal in life, that goal is pure, focused, bent 100 percent on loving God with all your heart, soul, mind, and strength.

Faith Is Transparent

Pure faith leaves no room for being fake, posing, or trying to look like what you are not—perfect. Faith is transparent, clear for all the world to see, because when your faith is in God and not yourself, you don't have to seem to have it all together. It can be really easy in the life of faith to feel like putting on a good show somehow benefits God. Like if you were to reveal your sins to people, then they would think you were a hypocrite, and we all know hypocrites are bad PR for God. So it can seem like a better choice to just fake it till you make it—in other words, to pretend like your life is rosy, like you are filled with joy, hope, and self-control. You feel like you have to act patient and kind, faithful and good in your own strength, though it's not what you are thinking or feeling on the inside, all so you can represent God well. But that's being fake, and it isn't having faith. Faith isn't fake because faith wants God to have free reign to work all things together for the good of those who love him (see Rom. 8:28). When we are too scared to be honest with people, too embarrassed to admit that we have failed in the past or that we are struggling in the present, then we put more value on impressing people than on having true faith in God.

We, Hayley and Michael, are very transparent about our sin. We will tell you anything you want to know because we believe that if we are afraid to admit our sin, we are afraid of what people will think, and that's a sign of pride, which is the beginning of all sin in our lives. But we're also adults who are fairly mature in our faith, and we work for ourselves so we can't get fired or expelled for being transparent. Believers who are young in their faith or young in life need to choose who they confess to wisely. But we also know and want you to know that Satan's goal is to keep sin in his arsenal, using it to destroy us. But **when you confess sin freely, naming it as sin and telling others how God saved you from it, then your past sin is used for**

good and Satan is defeated. Being fake and hiding all your faults and blemishes makes the enemy very happy, because then your healing and forgiveness cannot be a witness to others who might be struggling with the very thing that you have lived through and overcome through the power of the Spirit. For example, we know a young girl who struggled with anorexia for a few years. She is now free from its grip, but she is afraid to talk about it for fear of admitting the big mistake she made in serving her pride and desire for control. What she doesn't understand is that her past sin cannot be used for good as long is it remains hidden. How many others could learn from her mistakes if she would freely talk about the bondage she used to be in and how God got her out of it? **Fearing transparency is a sign of polluted faith**—polluted by the fear of people over God, by the pride of wanting to look like we have it all together. This is a fake faith, because it deceives those around us who are led to believe that we are perfect.

Looking like you have things all together, like you are perfect, is deceptive and can actually lead people to stumble. They stumble when they look at so many people around them who don't seem to have any problems and think there must be something particularly wrong with them because they sure aren't perfect or sin-free. In that state of mind they begin to not only hate their sin but

also condemn themselves, even to the extent of thinking that they are not good enough for God. But being
authentic, sharing both the good and bad parts of your
past, can actually encourage those around you because it
helps them to know they are not alone. And when you confess a sin that God has already forgiven and you have been
set free from, you give others hope, and we all need that.

As long as we keep our sin in the dark it remains useless,
unable to help or teach those around us. But if we walk in the
light—if we bring our sin out and let the world see it—then
we redeem our sin and use it for good. Confession, then, is
a beautiful part of pure faith. If you know God's Word then
you know there isn't anyone who doesn't sin, so there
should be no one who pretends to be sin-free, no one
who acts perfect. If you act like you are perfect, you are
calling God a liar and pretending to be something you
are not. But if you freely confess the sin in your life,
admitting those areas where you were impure in
your faith and coming clean with your messy life,
then the light of God shines on the dark places
and not only heals you but also offers hope to
those who see his work in you.

If your life has been impure in any area
and you are seeing that through the help
of the Holy Spirit, then it is time to admit
your impurity and to turn away from it.
You cannot live in Christ while you live
in sin, and you cannot reveal the grace

of God to others while you hide the grace he's shown you. If you have confessed your sin and turned away from it, if you can claim God's amazing grace in your life, then share it with the world. Tell others of his great kindness and love. Don't keep it for yourself like a selfish child hiding a batch of cookies from the others, but open up the jar and let others see the goodness that could be theirs as well.

If you are currently stuck in some kind of sin and have not worked through the forgiveness and grace of God, then you can confess to him right now. Confess and be forgiven (see 1 John 1:9)! And if you feel that you need healing from that sin, then as we said in the beginning of the book, you can confess that sin to another righteous person (someone who loves God, speaks his Word, is mature, and can be trusted) and allow them to pray for you. In that God promises healing (see James 5:16). And after you have healed and God has taught you to turn away from your sinful past, you can begin to talk about the healing that you went through in your past and share it with others.

Being pure is about being authentic, not fake. It's about wanting Christ more than the appearance of having it all together. Get this: talking about your sin and seeking healing for it makes you pure! It's about allowing the light of God to shine brightly on your dark parts and to clean them, purifying them from all unrighteousness, so that the enemy has no hold on you and so that he cannot withhold any part of you from others. So let your sin be used for good by sharing the gift of God's forgiveness and grace with others through sharing your life in a genuine and authentic way.

Faith Is Surrendered

Pure faith is completely surrendered to the will of God. If you are not surrendered, then you continue to have to fight for the things you want. Without surrender the battle rages on and you will not win but fail. But when you surrender to someone, you stop resisting them. You stop pushing against them or pulling away from them, and instead you abandon yourself entirely to them. This is the image of true purity. **To be pure you must abandon yourself— heart, soul, emotions, dreams, hopes—to the One you were made for, God himself.** You empty yourself of all of your worldly attachments, all of the things that you used to believe were important or even essential for your life, and you abandon yourself, or die to yourself, in order that you might live for Christ.

In this dying to self you stop responding to the parts of you that resist God's call on your life. You stop listening to your self as it begs and pleads for what it wants, and you listen instead to the voice of the Holy Spirit that often contradicts your self-life. This is the act of surrender, and you cannot have a pure faith without it. But what does surrender look like in everyday life? That's an important question, especially because it's so unnatural to give in and abandon your life to someone else when your own voice is so loud and constant in your head. How do you surrender your life to God? Part of the answer to that question is found in Romans 12, where Paul tells us to "present your bodies as a living sacrifice, holy and acceptable to God, which is your spiritual worship. Do not be conformed to this world, but be transformed by the renewal of your mind, that by testing you may discern what is the will of God, what is good and acceptable and perfect" (vv. 1–2). This passage confirms what we saw in chapter 3, which is that surrender has to do with turning over your body as a living sacrifice. You do that by giving up any claim on it—that is, by determining that your body isn't your own to use as you will but is meant for the express purpose of serving and bringing glory to God. We've been over that enough already, so now it's important that we read on to the second half of this passage, which gives us the very important call to no longer be conformed to this world but to be transformed by the renewing of our minds (see Rom. 12:2).

This is an essential part of pure faith. When you are conformed to the world, you do things based on what the world deems acceptable. You go where the world says it's acceptable to go and do what the world says is acceptable to do. As you do this, your faith gets polluted, diluted, and contaminated. You start, if only subconsciously, to believe the lies the world calls truth (see 2 Cor. 4:4), and as you do you start to accept things in your life as just normal to the human condition—things like bitterness, resentment, a desire for revenge, fantasy, laziness, gluttony, harsh treatment of your body, materialism, worry, fear, isolation, gossip, lying, cheating, stealing, hating, busyness, obsessive-compulsiveness, cutting, drunkenness, lust, complaining, self-obsession, idolatry, and much more. These become "acceptable sins" to you, little emotional bumps in the journey of your life that you have learned to live with and even welcome despite knowing how God feels about them because you think, "What the heck, everyone does it." If that's how you see them, then you have not surrendered your life to God but to sin. Rather than renewing your mind by testing and discerning what is the will of God, you have been lazy and just accepted what the world has spoon-fed you as "truth lite," or what we call "acceptable sin."

This idea that things are okay because everyone else is doing them is at the root of much of the impurity in your life. But the surrendered life is a unique one. Not many people reach for it or achieve it because the notion is choked out by the voice of this world that screams in your ear from all kinds of places: friends, entertainment, fashion, books. But the surrendered life has such a desire for the things of God that it spends more energy hearing from him than from the world. Then when the world screams, the ears of the surrendered hear the lies behind its call and reject them immediately as untrue and therefore unfaithful.

You might think this idea of surrender sounds impossible. After all, you live in the world, you are surrounded by it all day long, so how can you possibly turn your back on it other than moving to some kind of monastery or something? The answer is the same as it has been for all of our talk on purity: you don't do it, but God does it for you. In Philippians 2:13 we discover that "it is God who works in you, both to will and to work for his good pleasure." So it isn't on your shoulders but rests on his. Your only work is to ask him for the strength to abandon yourself to him so that he might make your surrender complete. In doing this you choose God over the world, and you determine to set your mind on him and to respond to his voice rather than the world's. As you do this you will see things in your life change. You will begin to rearrange your world to get rid of bad influences and to gravitate toward godly ones. Your taste in music or TV shows might change. Your idea of entertainment might be different now. And your desire for certain stuff might be diminished if not removed completely. But it all comes not from your rugged effort or determination but from your giving in to the Spirit and letting go of all that contradicts him.

Faith Hopes

True purity in faith has a pure hope in Christ and nothing else to save you. When your hope is pure, it doesn't divide itself between two things, believing in them both to rescue you, to fulfill you, or to please you. That's the beauty of pure hope—that when it is undivided, resting solely on Jesus, you are never disappointed (see Rom. 5:5).

Hope is essential for the human mind. Hopelessness, like worldliness, leads to anger, bitterness, depression, hatred, and despair. **When you have nothing to hope in, you have nothing to live for.** You lose the desire to keep living. Thoughts of separation from the rest of the world can fill the mind of the hopeless. Even thoughts of ending it all can sound like relief to the mind that has no hope. We must hope in something; it's what we were made to do. But hope in anything other than God will always disappoint. That's why you hear so many stories of the rich and famous dying from drug overdoses, killing themselves to numb the pain of finding that the life they had always hoped for didn't give them what they dreamed it would.

But when your mind is set on the things of God—when you take your eyes off of the world and look up—you find so much to hope for. Knowing not only that God is all-powerful but also that he loves you more than anyone else in the universe and has good plans for your welfare and not for evil (see Jer. 29:11) is the best source of hope there is. Because God will never fail you, he will never lie or deceive you but will always come through on his promises, you can have hope. "Set your minds on things that are above, not on things that are on earth" (Col. 3:2), and you will find all the hope you will ever need. There are a lot of things you can hope in, but only one thing is worthy of your hope. When the people around you offer you hope, they either give you hope in God or hope in the things of this world. It's hard for people who are less spiritual than you to give you hope in God because they don't have as much hope as you. So they might give you hope in success, love, or popularity. They might keep your eyes on the prizes that man sees as valuable and distract you from the prize of heaven. If you find yourself hoping for the things of this world, check your friendships and see if you don't have someone who encourages this mis-placed hope in you and so influences you to be less than purely dedicated to God.

Michael's Impure Hope

When I was in school my main goal was getting married. I put all my hope in the marriage I would one day have. So when a girl came along who wanted me, I jumped at the chance to start a family, my dream life. But what I didn't know was that I had put so much hope in getting married that I didn't take the time to consider who I was marrying or who *I was* going into the marriage. The marriage soon broke down because I wasn't living for God and neither was she, and it ended disastrously in divorce, a fact I regret to this day. (Hear me now: Hayley is an amazing wife, more than I could ever have dreamed of! So I'm glad that even after that mistake, God led me to her.) But the hope that I should have put in Christ was placed in that relationship, so it's no wonder it ended. The fact that I wasn't living a life purely devoted to God but instead was devoted to pleasing myself is to blame for me divorcing instead of making it work.

There are a lot of things you can put your hope in. You can put your hope in money, friends, fame, or success. You can put your hope in something you really want and think that getting it will make your life better. But what or who you put your hope in has a lot to do with your purity. When your hope is in Christ and nothing else, when you look to him for your joy and your contentment, then your mind is pure because "everyone who thus hopes in him purifies himself as he is pure" (1 John 3:3). But as with everything that is divided, purity goes out the door when you divide your hope between God and something or someone else, when you put your hope for a better life elsewhere. Ephesians 4:4 says that we were "called to one hope" (NIV), not two or three. Not hope and the backup hope in case the first thing you hope for doesn't pan out but one hope, and that is the gospel of Jesus Christ (see Col. 1:23).

We aren't saying it's not okay to be hopeful—it is. You can hope to see your friend tomorrow. Hope to go to college. But when you *put your hope* in something, you believe that something will make or break your life. Think about the basketball player who puts all his hope into getting an NBA contract. He devotes most, if not all, of his life to the sport, practicing it, studying it, and serving it with the hope that one day it will bring him all he ever wanted. This putting your hope for joy, peace, comfort, contentment, acceptance, forgiveness, or anything that God himself provides in the wrong thing is impure hope that pollutes the mind of the believer. Can you be successful in sports, medicine, or anything else without putting your hope in it? That's something only you can answer. But this we can say: when God calls you to put your hope in him, he wants you to put your hope fully on him and not divide it with another. "Therefore, preparing your minds for action, and being sober-minded, set your hope fully on the grace that will be brought to you at the revelation of Jesus Christ" (1 Pet. 1:13).

When your hope is purely set on God you are never hope-less, because God never disappoints. Even if things look bad to everyone else and your heart wants to agree, pure faith doesn't lose hope because God can be trusted. In Romans 5 this idea is spelled out. First we see the results of faith: "Therefore, since we have been justified through faith, we have peace with God through our Lord Jesus Christ, through whom we have gained access by faith into this grace in which we now stand" (Rom. 5:1–2 NIV). Here we see that your faith comes before your justification and peace with God. Then comes a hope that is the result of not glory and success but faith through tri-als and tribulation. Check it out: "And we rejoice in the hope of the glory of God. Not only so, but we also rejoice in our sufferings, because we know that suffering produces perseverance; perseverance, character; and character, hope. And hope does not disappoint us, because God has poured out his love into our hearts by the Holy Spirit, whom he has given us" (Rom. 5:2–5, NIV 1984). So when you have faith in God, suffering produces perseverance, not stress and worry, and perseverance builds your character, and character increases hope. And all because your faith was not divided.

Hopelessness leads to all kinds of trouble. It leads to depression (see 1 Thess. 4:13), to fear (see 2 Cor. 3:12), to doubt (see Heb. 11:1), and to compromise (see Matt. 6:24). Without hope your faith is impure, divided, tainted with sin. But when you can hope even in the things you cannot see (see Rom. 8:24), your heart has no need to be troubled, because hope fills it with the certainty of victory, even if not until you reach heaven (see Col. 1:5). If you feel hopeless, then it's time to find your hope. It is an impure faith that finds nothing to hope for. When hopelessness grabs hold of you, you have to reject it as deceit and begin to speak truth to yourself. Hopeless thoughts are impure because they accuse God of lying to you—that is, they argue against his Word. So they have to be stopped in their tracks. You can do that by rejecting them and replacing them with truth from Scripture. Take a look at this list of the hopeless lies that you might be believing and their remedy found in Scripture:

Lies	Truth
"I'm not good enough for God to love."	You don't have to be good for God to love you (see John 3:16; Gal. 2:16; Eph. 2:4–5, 8).
"My life will be miserable until I get what I want."	If you believe only getting what you want will make you happy, then you are letting your circumstances control you (Phil. 4:11–12).
"I can't handle rejection."	Any rejection God allows in your life is meant to teach you something (see James 1:2–4). Will you learn your lesson or allow it to destroy you?
"Life is never going to get better."	It is only faith, not doubt, that will allow you to see God's hand in your life and so see his love and faithfulness in everything (see Rom. 1:17; 5:1–2; Heb. 11:1, 6).
"God will never forgive me."	God will forgive any of his children who ask him for forgiveness (1 John 1:9).
"My heart is broken."	Your heart isn't broken, just alive. If your heart couldn't break, then it would be hard, and a hardened heart is a dead heart (see Matt. 5:4).
"It would be better if I were dead."	For the believer things will be better once we are dead, but they will be the best if you persevere until God takes your life (Rom. 5:3–5; Heb 12:1–2).
"No one will ever love me."	Someone already loves you. He loved you enough to die for you (see Eph. 2:4–10).
"I will always fail."	God is for me and God never fails. He is for me even in my trials (see Ps. 136:1; Rom. 8:31; 1 Pet. 5:10).
"Suffering is senseless."	Suffering is essential to the life of faith. Suffering is meant to perfect you, not destroy you (see Rom. 5:3–5; 8:28).
"I can't survive the pain."	You can survive the pain with the help of God. Without him you may fail, but leaning into him and trusting him is the sure way to survive well (see 2 Cor. 1:3–4).
"No one loves me."	The only One you need loves you and will never leave you (see Heb. 13:5).
"I shouldn't bother trying since I'll just fail."	Whether you succeed or fail is up to God, so your only job is to continue to try. Trust him to be your success (see James 4:15).
"God demands too much of me."	God only demands of you what he is willing to help you to do (see Eph. 2:10).
"I just can't control myself."	The Holy Spirit helps you to be self-controlled; that's why self-control is a fruit of the Spirit (see Luke 18:27; Gal. 5:22–23; 2 Pet. 4:7 ESV). God wouldn't have commanded it if it were impossible.

All of these untrue thoughts and feelings make no room for the healing power of faith in God. They all make no room for God but instead focus on the things of this world. Many believers have these thoughts because they have allowed their feelings to trump the truth about God. If you find yourself thinking any of these lies, then it's time to inform your feelings of the truth. Dig into God's Word to find out what he says and who he is. Discover the truth about suffering and pain, which is that he uses it for good, and quit believing the lie that none of it makes sense and all is destructive. Pure faith doesn't accept the lies of the world but always hopes in the person and the Word of God.

Faith Prays

If your faith is less pure than you'd like it to be, then prayer is the answer. There's a verse in Jeremiah that you probably haven't seen in any other book on purity, or on any subject for that matter. It's kind of unexpected, and that's why we like it. It gives some good insight on prayer and the value of it to your faith, and it goes like this: "The shepherds are stupid and do not inquire of the Lord; therefore they have not prospered, and all their flock is scattered" (Jer. 10:21). Why are the shepherds called stupid here? Because they didn't inquire of, or look to, God for help. They didn't pray. When your faith is in God rather than yourself or other people, then you find it necessary to pray. After all, God is sovereign over everything; he is the one who moves mountains and places kings in power; if you have faith in him, why wouldn't you go to him for all of your needs?

Unfortunately, maybe your prayer hasn't been as powerful as you had hoped. In fact, it's often weak and boring. You pray out of duty rather than passion, if you pray at all. Sometimes it's just an afterthought or a quick Hail Mary before everything falls apart. But prayer was meant to be so much more. When your faith is pure, when it's all focused on God, your prayer is the same way. The trouble with prayer for most of us is the impurity of our prayers, which comes from either the subject of our prayers or our lack of prayer altogether.

In 1 Thessalonians 5:17 we are told to "pray without ceasing." When we fail to pray even thirty minutes a day, how can we say that we are praying continually? **Prayer is your vital link to the Father; it is the foundation of your devoted heart.** You can't devote yourself to God and get to know him one short meeting at a time. **God doesn't shower his gifts on the casual or hurried visitor.** Spending lengths of time alone with God is what encourages pure faith. Devoting not a portion of your heart to him but all of it leads to pure faith, as God says in Jeremiah 29:13: "You will seek me and find me, when you seek me with all your heart." **You cannot seek him with all your heart in your spare time.** That is seeking him with a part, not the whole. Each day you are given a set amount of hours to get things done, and how much you get done isn't as reliant on what you do as it is on how you pray. There are many schools of thought on prayer, and this book isn't big enough to cover them all, but consider this in your life of true purity: if you start your day off with prayer, you start everything out on a pure foot. But if you postpone your prayer and instead give way to the busyness of the day, those things you deem more urgent than waiting on God and listening to his voice will set the tone for the day.

When your heart is set purely on the Father—when he is your number one, number two, and number three goal—then you are compelled to get up in time to give him the first part of your day. It's not the getting up early that leads to the purity of your faith but the fact that getting up early breaks the chains of self-indulgence and strengthens not only your desire for God but your devotion to him as well. When God wants to meet with you in the morning he wakes you, if only for a second, and your choice is to roll over and ignore him or to feed your desire for him by denying yourself and getting up. As we read in Isaiah 50:4,

"Morning by morning he awakens; he awakens my ear to hear as those who are taught." If you are willing to ask God to wake you in time to rest with him before you start your day, he will do it, but you must respond as the psalmist did when he said, "Satisfy us in the morning with your steadfast love, that we may rejoice and be glad all our days" (Ps. 90:14). When you do, your faith will become clearer and clearer as the residue of selfishness is washed away by time in his presence.

The truth is that you can respond to the Spirit and follow him only by continually praying. When prayer ceases, your mind wanders back to the matters of the flesh, but when you continually pray, your mind is set on the things of the Spirit and so follows his voice and responds to his will. Of this God says, "Blessed is the one who listens to me, watching daily at my gates, waiting beside my doors. For whoever finds me finds life and obtains favor from the Lord, but he who fails to find me injures himself; all who hate me love death" (Prov. 8:34–36).

Another problem with much of your prayer is the subject of that prayer. This is explained by James when he says, "When you pray for things, you don't get them because you want them for the wrong reason—for your own pleasure" (James 4:3 GW). That's talking about impurity. When your focus is yourself rather than God, you fail to abide in Christ, and as you fail to abide, your prayers become impure. But if you abide in Christ, thinking as he thinks and walking as he walks, then you will live in him and God will answer your prayers because they will be in agreement with his will. As we see in John 15:7, "If you live in me and what I say lives in you, then ask for anything you want, and it will be yours" (GW).

Prayer is a part of faith; without it your faith is polluted, weak, and toxic rather than healthy and pure. But the springs of your heart can run clear and clean if you devote your heart to much prayer—not prayer that is done out of obligation but prayer that flows out of love. When you love someone you want to be with them, listen to them, and talk to them, and the same is true for God: the more you love him, the more you will desire to be with him. Maybe until now you haven't realized his desire to be with you. Maybe you haven't heard his quiet call in the mornings asking you to come and watch for him. If not, then do not fret but listen. See if he isn't calling you to a life of purity. See if he isn't wanting all of your heart and all of your mind, even the part that covets its sleep early in the mornings. Remember, you can survive better without nourishment than you can without fellowship with God. If your spiritual life is anemic and weak, then get to the source of your strength by praying.

Hayley's Impure Prayer

Every morning God wakes me up. I haven't used an alarm clock in ten years. It's usually very subtle. I roll over and see the clock says 4:30, and I have choices to make. I can close my eyes and rest a bit more, or I can get up, open my Bible, devote my day to God. I must confess that many times I resist him and stay in bed, but when I do, my life becomes a struggle. Now, I'm not saying you should get up early so things will go better in your life, but the truth is that the struggles of our lives directly reflect the purity of our hearts. When you rise early to meet with God, the rest of your day is set fully on God, and as you live in the place you were meant to live, things inevitably go better. It isn't a matter of using prayer to improve your day but a matter of purifying your day by starting it with prayer. We can't let our prayerlessness cause feelings of guilt, because God's grace is big enough to forgive us, but we can use those feelings of conviction to drive us closer to the giver of life.

The pursuit of purity is less about what you do and more about what God does. Don't miss out on the truth about purity: it isn't just about avoiding you-know-what but is about giving yourself in total abandon to the One who loves you more than anyone else. Purity starts in your heart before it affects your body. If you don't get to the root of your purity in the state of your heart, then not only will the purity you desire in your physical life be spiritually useless but its very existence will be in jeopardy. The truth is that without the Holy Spirit informing your mind, you cannot truly ever be pure. The nonbeliever may reach for purity of body or mind, but in order to be pure they must give themselves to the One who cleanses and purifies our souls. Since purity is defined as giving all of yourself to God, it requires the call of God on your life. As we learn from Jesus in John 15:16, "You did not choose me, but I chose you and appointed you that you should go and bear fruit and that your fruit should abide, so that whatever you ask the Father in my name, he may give it to you." The person with no faith cannot bear the fruit of purity, because it grows from a life lived in Christ.

A Final Word

When we were young we knew little of the pure life. Instead we strived to look good, to be happy, and to do our best to obey God's "rules." But when we grew in love for God, we started to grow in faith, and as our faith in him grew, our faith in ourselves weakened. The result wasn't low self-esteem but high God-esteem. As our love for God informed our decisions, we sought to please him instead of ourselves, and the purity we had compromised returned. We began to love him with all of our heart, soul, mind, and strength. As we grew in faith we stopped allowing our lives to be controlled by lies and started to check everything against the truth of God's Word. Things like love and community, hope and faith started to look different to us as we saw God's heart on the matter. And as we began to believe and to trust that faith in him was all that was required, we were set free from the life of bondage to effort, strain, and struggle. We were set free to live a life of true love and true purity.

If you want a pure life—if you are ready to love God with everything and to abandon yourself fully to him—then let today be the day. Turn away from the things of this world and look to Jesus, the author and perfecter of your faith (see Heb. 12:2). Thank him for revealing truth to you and for giving you his Holy Spirit to guide and protect you. Your purity depends on him—no, your purity *is* him! Remember what we said in the introduction: if you have accepted Christ as the Lord of your life, God sees you as pure because of Christ's shed blood and his Spirit in you. And as the Spirit works in your life, he moves you to become more and more like him, to have the mind of Christ. In other words, you don't start pure and hold on so you don't lose it; you start out as a sinner in need of Christ's purity, and then you are changed over time to become like him. And all the while, God sees you as pure because of his Son. No longer look for purity anywhere else but in his hands. Put yourself there and be free. Let go of the world and dive in headfirst to the pure waters and words of the gospel. They are refreshing and safe, and they will give you all that you need to live a pure life.

Notes

1. Dietrich Bonhoeffer, *Life Together: The Classic Exploration of Faith in Community* (New York: Harper-One, 1978), 17–18.

2. Amy Carmichael, *If: What Do I Know of Calvary Love?* (Fort Washington, PA: CLC Publications, 2003), 46.

3. Andrew Murray, *The Master's Indwelling*, available online at the Christian Classics Ethereal Library, http://www.ccel.org/ccel/murray/indwelling.html.

4. Dietrich Bonhoeffer, *The Cost of Discipleship* (New York: TouchStone, 1995), 89.

5. A. W. Tozer, *The Knowledge of the Holy* (San Francisco: HarperSanFrancisco, 1961), 2.

Hayley DiMarco is founder of Hungry Planet, where she writes and creates cutting-edge books that connect with the multitasking mind-set. She has written and co-written numerous bestselling books for both teens and adults, including *God Girl*, *Devotions for the God Girl*, *Mean Girls*, *B4UD8*, and *Die Young*. Follow her on Twitter @hayleydimarco.

Michael DiMarco is the publisher and creative director of Hungry Planet. He has written and co-written numerous bestselling books for both teens and adults, including *God Guy*, *Devotions for the God Guy*, *B4UD8*, *Independence Day*, *Almost Sex*, and *Die Young*. Follow him on @Twitter dimarco.

Michael and Hayley live with their daughter in Nashville, Tennessee.

Become the Woman God Created You to Be

When you become a God Girl, your life will never be the same.

Available Wherever Books Are Sold

The Ultimate Bible just for the God Girl!

With special features like Ask Yourself, Prayers, God Girl Stories, and Know This Devotions, all written by bestselling author Hayley DiMarco, the *God Girl Bible* is a must-have for girls thirteen and up! If you're ready to grow closer to God, grow in your faith, and join an on-line group of girls from around the globe growing together, the *God Girl Bible* is for you!

Available Wherever Books Are Sold

Become the Man God Created You to Be

When you become a God Guy, your life will never be the same.

Available Wherever Books Are Sold

The *Ultimate Bible* just for the *God Guy!*

Combining the clear everyday language of GOD'S WORD Translation with inspirational writing from bestselling author Michael DiMarco, the *God Guy Bible* is jam-packed with timeless features.

Available Wherever Books Are Sold

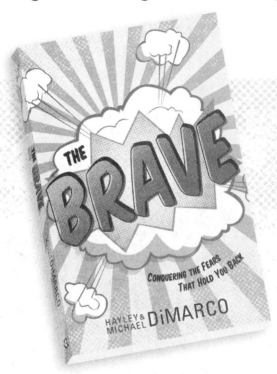

Breaking free from the things that consume you

Are you obsessed? We can all feel that way at times—when every bit of our thoughts, time, and energy are poured into something all-consuming. But those things can get between you and God. Hayley will show you how putting things in their proper place helps you become rightly obsessed with God.

Available Wherever Books Are Sold

Dating or waiting?
First date or 500th?

Hungry Planet tells you everything you need to know.

Available Wherever Books Are Sold